André Previn

Edward Greenfield

Drake Publishers Inc

NEW YORK

ISBN 0–87749–527–0

Library of Congress Catalog Card Number 73–4710

Published in 1973 by Drake Publishers Inc
381 Park Avenue South, New York, N.Y. 10016
© Edward Greenfield 1973

Printed in Great Britain

❧ Contents ❧

❧ *Foreword* ❧

by the Rt Hon EDWARD HEATH, MBE, MP

In this book, Edward Greenfield gives an account, at once sympathetic and clear-eyed, of André Previn's career and of his recording achievements. He shows how Previn's success is based on a phenomenal variety of experience as pianist, arranger, composer and conductor. By the time he was four he was playing the piano; by the time he was fourteen he was in business as an orchestrator. Before he left school, he was writing music for films; before he was twenty, he was not only a national success as a jazz pianist in the United States, but he was also conducting the MGM Orchestra in his own film scores and learning the standard repertory with rehearsal groups made up of players from the Hollywood film companies' orchestras.

To have achieved so much so early augurs immense vigour and an insatiable capacity for hard work. It has also served to make Previn an extremely professional musician: an indispensable quality in a conductor who wishes to earn and retain the respect and affection of a first-class symphony orchestra.

Edward Greenfield also catches the personal qualities which are familiar to André's friends and colleagues: his enthusiasm and zest, his restless vitality (which seems to drive him on occasion to the limit of his resources), his total lack of any kind of pomposity or conceit, and his natural gift for communication.

I came to know Previn when he first became associated with the London Symphony Orchestra and I was the Chairman of the LSO Trust. I had to give that up when I became Prime Minister, but I have tried to keep in touch with the orchestra and with André, and I accepted with pleasure (though with some apprehension) his invitation to conduct the orchestra in the opening work in its Gala Concert in November 1971. It was when he introduced me to the audience on that occasion that André suggested that, since I was taking over his job, he should take over mine, at least for the duration of the *Cockaigne Overture*: thus becoming one of the only two people I know who have publicly acknowledged a readiness to change jobs with me (the other would definitely like to do so for longer).

There is one mystery for which Edward Greenfield does not offer the solution, though he provides the facts. What is the origin of Previn's love of

England and his affinity for British music? How is it that a musician of Russian Jewish origin, of German and American upbringing, finds himself at home in the Surrey countryside, and in the music of Walton and of that most English of British composers, Vaughan Williams, all of whose symphonies he has now recorded?

Part of the explanation is no doubt that the way of life and the conditions of music-making in this country are congenial to him, as they have been to other distinguished muscians from abroad who have based their careers here. And yet there seems to be more to it than that: a spiritual affinity which dates back (as Edward Greenfield makes clear) long before he thought of making his home here and which lies deeper than anything that can be accounted for by social or musical circumstances.

I do not pretend to have fathomed the mystery. I am content simply to accept it, and its result, with gratitude. André Previn's presence enriches the world's musical life; may it long continue to do so.

10 *Downing Street, Whitehall*
November 1972

✣ *Introduction* ✣

As I warned André Previn when starting work on this book, the danger is that he will seem too good to be true. Here in an age of cabinned specialisation is a shining exception, the Compleat Musician, the man who seemingly without effort spans the different and often conflicting fields of music, creation as well as interpretation, playing as well as conducting, the segregated worlds of classic and pop, jazz and film; the man who appears on television and communicates in words just as immediately and vividly as he does in notes.

At this mid-point in his career it is worth noting that he is putting down roots in a way he has not previously managed in his extraordinarily varied life to date. A television interviewer actually asked him against the oak-beamed background of his Surrey home whether he was now becoming an English country squire. "Not with this accent I'm not", he returned quickly with a sharp American snarl, utterly incapable of being pompous, always ready to observe himself in half-amusement from outside.

That habit of self-observation goes—perhaps paradoxically—with an ability to remain unself-consciously himself in whatever situation. Anyone who has seen André Previn on television has seen the man exactly as he is to those around him. Few figures as much in the public eye as he make so little distinction between their public and private faces—maybe a reflection of his multicoloured background. If he talks to a passer-by in the same tones as he would to the Prime Minister, to a television comedian as he would to a member of the London Symphony Orchestra, it is because he is first and foremost a communicator—a communicator interested in communication in both directions, in receiving as well as giving. He actually listens far more than is common with people as gifted and articulate as he.

If he meets you off the train at his local station in Surrey, you cannot help being struck by the superficial contradictions—the youthfully casual clothes worn by the man who chooses to drive a heavy maroon Rover with coach-lines down the side and a solid walnut-faced interior—an unostentatious old man's car. He has never in his life been interested in cars as status symbols, and either way the image is of secondary importance. In his timbered drawing room he will point to a row of four gold Oscars tucked high on a shelf near

Opposite: André Previn 1971.
[EMI/David Farrell

6

the ceiling in a dark corner. "I kind of half put them up", he explains, "it would be too self-conscious to hide them."

The house itself, built in 1728, is that of a well-heeled stockbroker. A swimming-pool, kidney-shaped, outside the back window gives a suggestion of Hollywood pretensions, but that was already there when Mia and he bought the house. They regarded the pool as on the whole a drawback, and have never swum in it. More bizarre, but much more personal to husband and wife, is the LNER railway guard's van painted in red and green standing on its own length of rail in the wood behind the house. It was one of André's highly original ideas for a birthday present to his wife, a sort of summer-house. In the local pub down the road Previn drinks pints of bitter like a true Englishman, and it was only his appearance on BBC Television with the comedians, Morecambe and Wise, at Christmas 1971 that made him a celebrity there.

In every one of a series of musical careers from the age of fifteen onwards he has had immediate and striking success. He has been married three times, and all three of his wives have themselves been formidably brilliant in their careers. Almost without trying he has been constantly in the headlines. Journalists will tell you that almost any words he utters spontaneously provide 'copy'.

But as I said, the question for anyone studying him as a serious musician must be: is he too good to be true? Can the deft Hollywood film composer and inventive jazz musician develop into a searching interpreter of Beethoven's Ninth Symphony? The age of specialisation tends to look suspiciously on the all-rounder, to distrust achievement in different fields, but this study of his life—the first yet published in book form—shows, I think, how even the most unlikely turns in his career have helped in his development as a great conductor, that the seeds of his later achievement were there from the start. His success—formidably witnessed by the already long list of his records—is based very clearly not on luck but on natural flair, innate musical talent, developed gradually through unremitting hard work in the most unconventional of musical trainings.

🌺 *The Life* 🌺

BERLIN TO LOS ANGELES

André Previn was born in Berlin on 6 April, 1929, the third and last child of Jack Previn and Charlotte Epstein, parents whose families had both reached Germany in the previous generation from Russia. Young Previn—only four when Hitler came to power—was brought up under the shadow of the rising Nazi movement. As he says today: "The reason I knew we were Jewish was a terribly simple and graphic one—they threw rocks at me."

Previn's father came from Alsace, torn between France and Germany. In Berlin the surname was spelled Prewin, but the part of the family that gravitated to the French side of the frontier preferred the spelling 'Previn', and André's first name reflects his father's dual allegiance. His mother too, though herself born in Frankfurt-am-Main, had close relations in France. André's second name was originally Ludwig (changed later on entry into America), and that he suggests is musically inspired like his elder brother's name of Wolfgang. "Interesting to choose Mozart before Beethoven", he says, but there Steve Previn, nowadays like André a British resident, presents a more down-to-earth explanation. Ludwig was the name of their father's best friend, just as Wolf (translated Wolfgang) was given to the first son in tribute to his paternal grandfather.

It was not an orthodox Jewish family, and André did not receive a conventional religious education. He was never confirmed and never went to synagogue, but after rocks started being thrown "even if you're dense, you begin to get the idea that you're different". André's earliest education was musical rather than religious. His father, a highly successful criminal lawyer and judge, was a devoted amateur musician, and though his first two children —Steve and his sister, Leonore, two years younger—showed no sign of musical talent, it did not take long before André's musical bent was discovered. At the age of four, his mother reports, he would beg to be allowed to stay up for the chamber concerts which his father and friends gave every week in the music-room of the Previn's comfortable penthouse flat. He would sit under the piano, and at 8.30pm on being told that it was already long past his bedtime, he would plead to hear just one more piece.

At four he was already playing the piano fluently, and elder brother and sister were banned from the keyboard in favour of the baby of the family.

9

André began to play duets, four-handed with his father, long before his feet could reach the pedals. To this day in Beethoven, Haydn, Mozart and Schubert symphonies, he still keeps in his mind the layout on the page of the duet arrangement, *primo* and *secondo*. Mrs Previn remembers that very early indeed one of her husband's friends played André a Chopin waltz, transposing it a semitone. On being asked how he liked it, the child was polite, but wondered why it was in the wrong key. His gift of perfect pitch was natural, not acquired.

André learnt to read exceptionally early, and his father would demonstrate his son's talent to friends by getting him to read Gibbon parrot-fashion. From then on he was a voracious reader. He remains so. His appetite for information is as catholic as his taste in music.

When André was five, his father took him to his first concert. Furtwängler was conducting the Berlin Philharmonic in Brahms, and the opening item, the Academic Festival Overture—a work to please a youngster so Previn senior thought—explained his choice. The rest of the programme was heavier—Brahms's Third and Fourth Symphonies. As Previn reports: "I loved it so much that I went home, was sick, and had to be put to bed, feverish." The following week his father, nothing if not logical after a Prussian legal training, decided to take his musical son to the opera, and then it was "a bizarre double bill"—a first half of Strauss's *Salome* (formidable enough for any five-year-old) followed by Delibes's *Coppélia* ballet. Again André enjoyed it all enormously, but "I got completely confused. For years I thought that *Salome* took place in a toyshop".

Below left: André Previn, aged 2.

Below right: André, a very youthful student at the Berlin Hochschule.

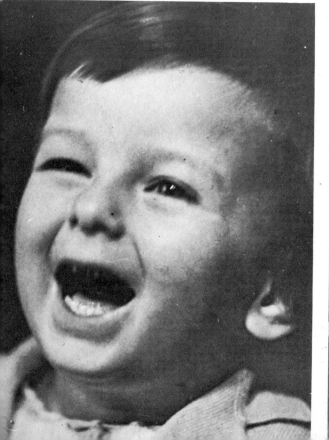

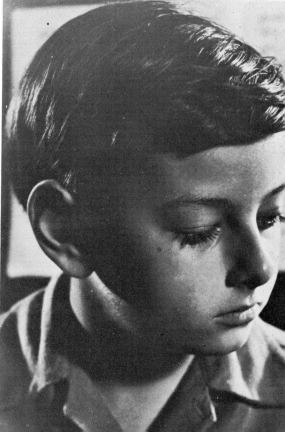

André's formal musical education had already started. As a pianist he progressed rapidly not just through lessons but through his father's daily habit of presenting him with music to sight-read, Haydn, Mozart, Beethoven or Brahms. "He would say 'Play it at tempo. Never mind mistakes or disasters, or whether you have to fake your way through. Read it!'" His father's idea was not so much to develop a prodigy as to ensure that his son would actually enjoy making music by being able to present it coherently and intelligibly from the start. The result was that André "never had to study these things. I just read them." His father's piano technique was not that of a professional, but he played 'with a combination of love and cunning', something he quickly conveyed to his son.

At the age of six André was taken by his father to the Berlin Hochschule, and there introduced to the head of the piano department, Professor Breithaupt, a venerable figure in his eighties revered by generations of Berlin musicians (years later George Szell could hardly believe that Previn could ever have had contact with so ancient a figure). Breithaupt at once recognised the child's talent as a pianist, but such was the rigidity of the Prussian system, even a six-year-old had to go through exactly the same course as those who entered the academy at a much later age. So it was he took not only lessons in piano but in theory, harmony, counterpoint, composition and musical history. Meanwhile for non-musical studies he was attending a private school in the prosperous district where the Previns lived, the Sickelschule, His fellow pupils still remember the phenomenal child pianist who could sight-read anything.

The Previn family in Berlin January 1934.

The political climate was by now affecting the lives of the Previn family. Steve Previn remembers rather more clearly than his younger brother the social tensions involved. German Jews, intensely patriotic, were convinced that Hitler represented only a passing phase, but even so Previn senior was persuaded by friends and family that it was no longer wise to ignore the possibility of fleeing from Germany. Young Stefan (Steve) was therefore dispatched to America, where in New York Mr and Mrs Jascha Heifetz were two of his principal guardian angels—the Heifetzes being long-established friends of the family. That foresight proved fortunate when later the whole family had to escape from Germany.

Of those days in Berlin André remembers in particular one Sunday when he and a friend took the elevated railway out into the country for a hike in the woods, taking sandwiches for their lunch ("all very German"). When they returned to the city, they found a torchlight procession starting. It was a day when the Nazis were organising a demonstration, and at the same time were rounding up all sorts of people indiscriminately. "I must have been a heartless little fellow," says Previn "because I don't remember the dread of it. I thought it all rather adventurous." The two youngsters watched the parade with bands of SS men carrying torches, and completely forgot the time. They were due home about 6 pm, and finally wandered in about 9.30 pm to find both sets of parents 'in extremis', resigning themselves to the fact that they had lost two children. There was no possibility for Jews then to ask the police for help. 'Too bad' would have been the answer.

André studied for three years at the Berliner Hochschule, riding off on his bicycle each morning but then one day the principal asked to see his father. Regretfully he explained that he could no longer afford to have a Jewish pupil in his academy, however talented. By then the family was already thinking seriously of leaving Germany, and this refusal of a musical education was, André feels, the straw that broke the camel's back. There was a quota system for leaving the country, but that meant a long delay. In the end a more drastic course had to be faced. André reports: "On the pretext of going on a weekend to Paris we just left everything—home, belongings, library, music and paintings. We went with no luggage. There was no war yet, and the Germans still did not prevent people from simply going away for the weekend. If you left with no money and no luggage, they presumed you were coming back, especially if you had as many belongings as my father did."

It was an ordinary flight from Berlin to Paris, but the Previns were one family among many who by this time in 1938, on the eve of the Munich crisis, were bent on fleeing from Germany in this desperate way. André remembers how intensive, even brutal, the customs search was before they left Germany. After the plane took off there was a rumour that it had been turned back and was returning to Germany. The tension was electric during the next two hours or so until the plane landed. No one spoke a word. And then when the plane was on the ground they waited for the officials to appear. André remembers to this day the extremity of relief as the door of the cabin opened, and an official called out in French: "Passports please!"

The Previns were fortunate in that Mrs Previn's brother was a professor at the Sorbonne. Also Jack Previn's Alsatian background meant that the family's allegiance was divided between France and Germany, and Uncle George was not the only relation they had to help them in their new exile. This uncle—who was later murdered by the Nazis in a concentration camp—was André's favourite relative. He even added the Christian name George to his own name in tribute when later he entered America. But relatives, however helpful, could still not protect the family totally from their extreme change of circumstances. From living in a penthouse in Berlin with servants and every luxury they went in Paris to what André describes as a hovel. Even so with the help of Uncle George there was little problem in getting the talented nine-year-old into the Paris Conservatoire to continue his musical studies with—among others—Marcel Dupré. He simply won a scholarship, and tuition was free. There, as in Berlin, it was still a question of studying a wide range of musical subjects, not just playing the piano. "I was shown other instruments, but I didn't take to them" he says. He also explains that it was only when later he reached California his really serious musical studies began. That of course is a relative statement. By most musicians' standards André Previn's training at the age of nine was very well advanced indeed.

Charlotte Previn looking at family photographs. [Edward Greenfield

The Previns were in Paris for just over a year. Already their son Stefan was established with friends in New York, and when in 1939 war threatened Europe, the family felt it was time to cross the Atlantic. Jascha Heifetz, who had acted as one of Steve's guardians in America, again came to their help. It was not possible simply to book a passage and leave France, and Heifetz it was who, as one of the family's two sponsors in America, arranged for them to bypass the immigration queue, which normally would have kept them waiting for up to four years. Fortunately the law firm to which André's father belonged had a branch in Paris, and that helped in the negotiations, which following Previn senior's ramrod rules of rectitude had to be "not even remotely illegal". As André explains: "My father was stuffily Prussian in observing the law". In California when the total means of the family was something like 15 dollars a week, he would make out his tax returns as though he was a Rothschild—absolutely to the penny. Mrs Previn was—and is—a more relaxed character. She herself is musical, but has little or no technical knowledge, and as André puts it her taste even today is "very conservative".

The Previns arrived in New York in the summer of 1939. It was then that officially the name was changed on their passports from its German form of 'Prewin'. As André says, like the relatives who were already established in America, they could hardly face the idea in an Anglo-Saxon country of regularly being called 'Proo-in'. So Previn they became, and André took this opportunity—as someone had explained to him he could—of having George as his middle name instead of Ludwig. The family's stay in New York brought a happy reunion with the elder son, Steve, but already they saw it was only to be a temporary stop. It was helpful that Steve, still at school, was already thoroughly Americanised and—most important—could speak English. The others, André, his parents and his sister, Leonore—or 'Lolo'—could between them speak hardly a word of English. André was able to play the piano regularly in New York but not to study seriously. It was left until they reached California after a hiatus of a month or so before André's education was continued.

They chose California for two reasons, one logical, one emotional. In the first place Charles Previn, 'Uncle Charlie', an uncle of André's father, was already established in Hollywood as the head of the music department of the Universal Studios. The other reason—which seems to have weighed even more formidably with André's father—was that when, soon after Hitler came to power, he had been thinking in rather abstract terms of leaving Germany he had seen one of the very first technicolor movies, *Ramona*, starring Loretta Young as the girl who falls in love with an Indian. In the middle of a frozen Berlin winter Previn senior sat watching in envy as Loretta Young consumed strawberries and cream on the porch of a sun-drenched California hacienda. That, he thought to himself, was where he wanted to go.

So it was they arrived in Los Angeles, but what had already become very evident was that Mr Previn's profession—of which in Germany he had been a leading practitioner—was going to be of no use whatever in providing any income for the family. He knew no English, and proved singularly in-expert at learning it. Where exiled doctors from Germany at once earned fortunes in America, the other Jewish refugees from the professional class, the lawyers, had an almost insoluble problem to face. Even granted a knowledge of English, it would have meant starting from scratch at law school, if Previn senior was going to become a lawyer under the American system and practise again. "In the meantime", as André comments, "we had to eat."

Fortunately Jack Previn was able to use his skill in music to get going again. As the benign old German music-teacher (he was still in his forties, but the image was there) he was happily able to cash in on what Steve Previn describes as Hollywood snobbery, where children have to have professional instructors for everything—even, according to one hoary chestnut, in tree-climbing. Mr Previn was not by nature patient enough (particularly not after helping to train the lightning-talented André) to be a good music teacher, but the message went round effectively: "He must be good, because he can't speak English properly". The financial return from giving piano lessons was poor, even after the initial contacts were made, and it did not help that the Previns with their European outlook did not know how to pretend to be richer than they were. Then and later Mr Previn rigorously turned his back on such things as hire purchase, though over the period from leaving France he had been forced to borrow from friends and relatives.

It was only after his arrival in California that André started to learn English. In New York he had not even been to school, but once in California his father determined that the only possible course for him was to sink or

swim, sending him to the local school. The first day, as André says, was one of "endless madness". He describes the occasion. "No one had told the teacher that I didn't speak any English. I had a brown paper bag with a sandwich in it, and she told me to put my lunch on the shelf at the back of the room. I smiled eagerly, and nodded at her and just sat there. 'Didn't you hear me' she snapped (or so he was told later) and again I just nodded at her. Before I knew what was happening I was being screamed at, and I didn't know what to do. So finally (kids being superficially cruel but basically nice) when the laugh was over, they explained things to the teacher. My father was right. I did learn English terribly quickly."

Not only did André learn English quickly, he soon found that with German education more intensive than American, he was still ahead of his contemporaries in the American system despite all the upset of moving from Berlin to Paris and through New York. That stood him in good stead later. More immediately, to help the family budget, or at least to get himself some pocket money and buy books and records, he set about finding odd jobs. He persuaded a downtown department store called Barker Brothers that he would be good at demonstrating their electric organs on the sixth floor. "I would go there after school from four to six till closing and sit there playing that kind of meaningless drivel which I suppose is played on electric organs at home, kind of 'By a waterfall'." That would bring him in the lavish sum of $1.50 for two hours, very useful for a penniless twelve-year-old. He also earned $2 dollars a session playing the piano in a dancing academy for well-bred little boys and girls.

After a time he found a job playing the piano in a silent film cinema. In Hollywood this had become something of a cult, and so in the manner of the 'twenties André would improvise appropriate music. At least it was intended to be appropriate. The climax of his career came when D. W. Griffiths' classic film *Intolerance* was being shown, with its brisk cutting between biblical times and the brazen 'twenties. "At one point I thought they had settled into a nice long sequence of Charleston-dancing flappers, and I swung whole-heartedly into *Tiger Rag*. The next thing I saw was the manager, apoplectic, storming down the centre aisle." What André had failed to notice in his enthusiasm was that the scene had changed to the Crucifixion.

It was about this time that Steve Previn graduated from Hollywood High School, and then with the help of Uncle Charlie went to be a messenger at the MGM studios, so helping the still-strained family budget. Even to get that lowly job in the magic world behind the film studio gates you needed a 'connection'. Though André's introduction came from a completely different direction, it helped to have a name already known.

Once established in high school André was exceptionally fortunate in the ways he was able to expand his music-making. Already he had studied orchestration, and he found to his delight that his school had an orchestra which did not restrict its activities to Chaminade, but positively welcomed orchestrations by fellow pupils. He was also getting interested in jazz, and would copy out the cascades of notes in Art Tatum's jazz improvisations

Opposite.
Above: Rehearsing with the LSO before recording: Kingsway Hall, 1966. [*RCA Records*

Below: Preparing for the next take: an early session for RCA. [*RCA Records*

17

producing a tolerable if necessarily stiff imitation of the original. So it was that when he was 14 he was already orchestrating the annual revue show of his high school class from beginning to end, and writing much of the original music too. He had also started selling orchestral arrangements to the local radio station 'for laughable money'. They were quite content to get second-rate arrangements for which they paid second or third-rate money." But were his youthful arrangements really second rate? "I heard some of those things later: they were awful! I was determined to write every single thing I knew into every one. I didn't know how to leave well alone."

As a useful all-round pianist he was also helping with the California Youth Symphony, an extraordinary organisation founded by a studio violinist with a mission, Peter Meremblum. He had two youth orchestras, one for real youngsters, the other for those up to 18, and conductors as famous as Rodzinski and Mitropoulos would come along to help rehearse at the Saturday morning sessions. Meremblum's repertory was decidedly idiosyncratic, with Brahms symphonies much less favoured than obscure Russian works, some of which André has never been able to trace since. Learning how a youth orchestra worked from the inside was more important than he realised at the time, and it was here that he first took up a baton and conducted.

But his destiny of becoming a conductor was far from plain, if only because his use of his musical talents was more striking still in other directions. As well as helping to write and present his class's show at high school, he was taking part in all sorts of school music activities, and his piano accompaniments at the dancing academy led him to form a group with a drummer and a bass-player which played at private dances in the Los Angeles area. That broadened his outlook in bringing him into contact with much more experienced musicians in the pop world. There was a time when André was working in night clubs in Los Angeles and was still too young to drive himself home after the show. His parents or his brother Steve would have to go and collect him. Steve remembers one occasion, when on the way home André asked him what he thought of the new trombone player. Steve tried to get him to identify which that was, and André replied: "You know, the one in the red shirt." That player was in fact, Steve reports, the only black musician present, yet it never occurred to the un-colour-conscious André to identify him by his skin.

Even in Germany the pattern had been set with the Previns of parents and children exceptionally close together. But where the usual Jewish family network requires intimate contacts too with brothers, cousins and so on, that was not the Previn way, if only because both parents had preferred to keep the family unit on its own. Nor were the two elder children jealous of their brilliant young brother. They did not resent him, as they might well have done, even though Steve to this day has a lingering regret about the abandonment of piano lessons. On uninhibited party occasions the two brothers will even today play the child's piano duet which formed part of Steve's last piano lesson, something by Clementi or Diabelli, no one can quite remember any longer. Their sister, Leonore, was in many ways the focus of the family's sense of humour. Wit is a natural part of the Previn make-up, but she it was who drew it out most regularly, then and later.

Steve's early departure for America, years before the others crossed the Atlantic, meant not a lessening of bonds but an intensification. The trials they all went through brought them together still further. It also meant that there was little chance of direct jealousy developing between the brothers. If he was a failed musician, Steve confesses, he might have felt jealous. As it is, successful in the film business on the production side, he can only share in André's success. Besides, André was famous already in his early teens. Even before his success in the film and record world, the name André Previn was well known in the Los Angeles neighbourhood. It was plain already that the schoolboy possessed some sort of spark that set him apart. It may give some clue to the relationship of the two brothers and their sister that they used a family whistle, designed to summon attention in a crowded public place without alerting the whole world. The Previn whistle, inherited from their parents, was the first phrase of Beethoven's Eighth Symphony. Whether in Wilshire Boulevard or Piccadilly Circus André and Steve can still make contact with this signal.

Even before he left high school, André had established himself as a professional writer of film music. His arrangements for the local radio station, not to mention his playing of jazz at the piano, helped to bring his name up when MGM decided that it was time for their pianist film-star, José Iturbi, to play some jazz in his next film. "Musicals usually included him playing the start of the Tchaikovsky piano concerto, accompanying Judy Garland in something and smoking a lot of pipes, so they wanted to lighten his image. But he was incapable of improvising anything. Someone told them that I was classically trained, and knew my way around jazz."

"The idea was that he was going to play—God help us—jazz variations on *Three Blind Mice*. So I wrote a piano version, José liked it a lot and they said 'We'll orchestrate it', because in those days it was not enough to play the piano without having at least sixty men behind you." The 15-year-old offered to do the orchestration too, and his offer was accepted if only because it meant one less fee. So it was that for the climax of his high school career André Previn led what he has since described as a "surreal life". He would finish high school at 3.30 in the afternoon and go on a series of three buses out to MGM. He would then progress to one of the rehearsal halls and see what was going on, and be given a number to arrange and orchestrate. His brother, Steve, was already working as a cutter in the studios, and was able to give his kid brother a few tips on the studio organisation and how to get around.

Not that André needed much instruction before he found his own way. He would return home from the studio about 7.30 pm, do his school homework and then get down to doing his orchestration of the evening. Up in the morning to school, out at 3.30 and off to the studio and so on round the clock. MGM also suggested that he might like to finish his education at the school which the studio provided for child actors of various ages—Elizabeth Taylor, Margaret O'Brien, Butch Jenkins and so on. Tempted for a moment, he refused, realising what sort of schooling would be provided and knowing what rewards there were among his contemporaries at a normal high school.

On top of all his other activities he was taking composition lessons. His principal teacher was Mario Castelnuovo-Tedesco, to whom he went on a scholarship, and he also had lessons from Joseph Achron and Ernst Toch. It is an understatement to say that at 15 he was doing at least two jobs at once. As Steve Previn says, André seemed to jump from being a child to being a man. He had not time for being a teenage youth. André himself, talking of his 'surreal' period before he finally left school, sums it up: "I adored it. I thought it was the best fun anybody ever had."

THE WORLD OF HOLLYWOOD

"The facile thing is simply to regret all those years, and make fun of the movie business." Even as he says that, André Previn knows perfectly well that his experience as a film arranger and composer formed a necessary stage in his development. His very success in his film work, coupled as it was with equal success as a jazz pianist, has inevitably led to doubts about his claims as a serious conductor. Yet not only did his youthful training under the considerate guidance of an intensely musical father give him a grounding in the classical tradition as thorough as any musician could want, his work in the film studios gave him a practical knowledge of orchestral work in all its aspects which any aspiring conductor looking at his career today must deeply envy. The facile thing would indeed be to regret the years in the film world. The wise thing—which ultimately involved a great deal of courage—was to use those years as a training, and then, unlike so many who have buried themselves for ever in Hollywood, break away when it was still possible to do so.

The day he left high school André had a ready-made job waiting for him in the MGM studio. As a *New Yorker* profile sarcastically put it, he got his job "after a one-day struggle to succeed". The fact remains that in his year of commuting between school and the studio, he had amply proved his professional skill. He was still a fairly lowly animal in the MGM music department, but that was the time in 1946 just after the war, when "every film was a success", and a studio like MGM had fifteen films in production simultaneously all the time. Each film demanded plenty of music—it was before the days, as Previn puts it, when "a film score consists of a hit number repeated eighty times"—and with orchestras of 60 musicians each, there was an insatiable demand for musical skill. Though there were star composers and arrangers in plenty, "they still needed real workhorse people on whom to load all the nonsense. It was necessary but unglamorous. If two people sat in a café for seven minutes, music had to be written for that, and if a procession went by, someone had to write the brass band music."

Opposite.
Above: With Leonard Bernstein.

Below: Rehearsing with Isaac Stern.

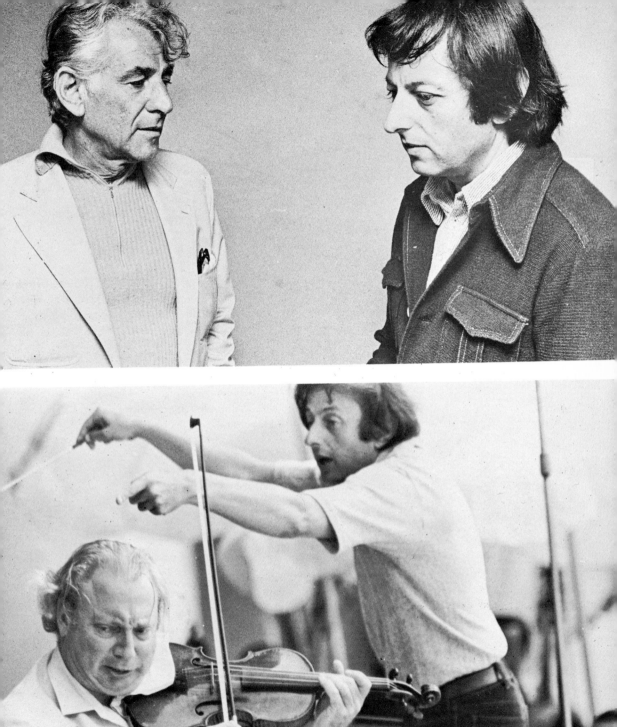

That was where the eager young recruit came in, not nearly important enough as yet to get a credit on film titles, but paid simply to fill in and do the donkey work for those who were established. Quite a few Hollywood composers still remained active "whose claim to composition rested solely on their ability to whistle little tunes to more sophisticated souls who could then write them down, develop them and orchestrate them". One of those for whom André worked was "a kind, nice man whose lack of musical knowledge was awe-inspiring. He was the only man I ever met who played the piano not with one finger but with just one thumb. It was creepy to watch." When gently André tried to tell him on one occasion that trumpets could not reach an octave and a half above high C, he simply retorted "Well, try, kid!" and withdrew.

Another composer, equally amiable, for whom André ghosted was Herbert Stothart, who had written successful operettas in the 'twenties, looked immensely distinguished with leonine white hair, but who "had absolutely no idea about the technique of music". His idea of writing a film score was to tinkle out a few old-fashioned melodies, and leave the rest to his 'ghost'. In one film over which André collaborated with him, he provided "an innocuous little melody", and then suggested that his ghost might use it for the title music with orchestration on the lines of Respighi's *Pines of Rome*. "It was great fun", Previn reports, piling the layers on and adding an organ for good measure, but when Stothart came to conduct it he still had to use a simple melody sheet following the principal melodic line, as he could read only the treble clef. While Stothart conducted, André sat at his feet on the podium, ready to point out errors and answer questions from any of the players. On this occasion Stothart launched into his title music with abandon, and when the whole studio was awash with sound and his arms were flailing like a windmill, he leaned down to André and in a delighted whisper, asked: "Did *I* write this?"

There were, Previn insists, plenty of excellent composers in Hollywood working 52 weeks a year and doing a keenly professional job—Miklos Rosza, Alex North, David Raksin and others—but even they were severely hampered by the lack of musical knowledge or even sensitivity of the producers. Also, each composer tended to get type-cast in a particular genre—horror film, Biblical epic and so on. Previn cherishes the memory of a notice that graced the walls of the MGM music department from 1936, after one movie tycoon had been listening to a new score on the set and noted a passage he did not like. He had asked about it and had been told that it was based on a minor chord. The following day a notice went up on the music department wall to the effect that 'from the above date no MGM score will contain a minor chord'. The inmates were so delighted with the absurdity of it they kept it framed in a place of honour.

Previn also tells the story of a film where the hero and heroine had to attend a chamber music concert, and the producer suggested "something with piano". André put forward the idea of a piano quintet ("Now, a quintet is a harp and what else?" asked the producer) and went on to record the first movement of the Schumann Quintet with the principals from the MGM Orchestra. The producer was delighted with the results. "It's so pretty", he said, "but I think we're wasting our time doing it this way. I want you to do it with a full orchestra." André argued, was shouted down by the producer, refused point blank to do what was asked, and was taken off the film. A pity perhaps he did not salve his conscience by thinking of Schoenberg arranging Brahms's Piano Quartet for orchestra.

Within a year André "was not making a fortune, but making more than a seventeen-year-old has any right to". He bought a suede coat, and a convertible, and dated his fair quota of chorus-girls. "Who's going to resist that?" he asks now. "Who's going to say: 'I'm sorry but I'm learning the *Hammerklavier*'?" He was lucky in being sponsored by a number of influential musicians, Johnny Green for example. Once a producer had used him on a film, and found him easy to work with, he was used again, and so his reputation built up remarkably quickly. It was also a wonderful training for anyone wanting to learn the finer points of orchestration. He is grateful that instead of having a conservatory teacher simply telling him that a particular passage would not sound well for so many reasons, he was able actually to hear his scoring realised by the very best professionals within the week. "I would sit on the scoring stage, dead tired, ticking off moments in my score and telling myself: 'No, that's awful; yes, that's all right; no, never do that again!' and so on."

The atmosphere of the studios at this time, Previn reports, was strange. It was "the last gasp of the big studios", yet most people there had no inkling that it would ever stop. They had a continuing sense of well-being, misplaced confidence that the good time would go on, that the false glamour and excitement were permanent qualities. It would have taken a very different character from André Previn to reject it all immediately whatever he came to think later, and certainly it would be hard to think of any lively teenager who had had immediate success in this milieu turning his back on it immediately. As it was, he found his companionship—chorus-girls apart—not among his direct colleagues in the music department, the composers and orchestrators, but among the performing musicians, some on the jazz side, some on the classical.

He was already a national success as a jazz pianist. His patient imitations of Art Tatum had led to more and more public performances, night-club engagements and so on, in the Los Angeles area, and already even before he had had his name on a film score, he had made his first jazz piano records, a series of singles in 1945 and 1946, and then a full LP, for RCA, a disc "which is now luckily out of print", as he says. Much to everyone's surprise the LP was a runaway success and sold something like 200,000 copies, which meant that he was asked to do another, and even when that did not repeat the success of the first, he was invited back for more recording sessions." I chased the success of that first album for about ten years and I only hit it about twice more; but anyway I was suddenly in the curious position of having a commodity at my finger-tips which made money."

The teenager's ability to make money meant that the Previn household

Right: Off to America for the LSO's 1972 tour. [Mary Lawrence

Below: Previn sets the fashion: rehearsing with the LSO on the US tour of 1972. [Mary Lawrence

was no longer in penury, far from it, for André's brother Steve was by now well-established too in the film world. His sister, Leonore, had become a vigorous Zionist in Beverley Hills, and when the state of Israel was established, she meditated for some time, and then decided to go there and live on a kibbutz. But then some eighteen months later, with equal strength of mind, she returned explaining that it had been a mistake, that she was a bad picker of oranges, that she hated cleaning fish, and that she would be of far more use to the Zionist cause, living her life in Beverley Hills with her family. As Steve explains, she was always "the gravital centre of the family", and her return was welcome to them all.

André's father never quite accepted the pop orientation of his musical son's career. He did not specifically say that André was betraying his art. "He was very, very good and fair about it since it didn't involve practising. I am sure if I had had rehearsals with groups in our house, he would have hated it." But at this early eruptive stage of André's career Jack Previn was able to take consolation in some of the more serious music-making that his son was somehow or other finding time to include in his incredibly busy schedule. For one thing he was continuing his composition lessons with Castelnuovo-Tedesco. Through the principal cellist in the MGM Orchestra, Willem Vandenberg—who was also associate conductor of the Los Angeles Philharmonic for a while—André was introduced to Joseph Szigeti, who at that time was living in the Palos Verdes district of the city. Szigeti wanted someone to play through difficult modern scores on the piano, and André's sight-reading ability had won him a phenomenal reputation even among the hundreds of skilled musicians at MGM. After one "particularly rough" session, Szigeti suggested that he, André and Vandenburg should play a Beethoven Trio. He asked André to choose, and was horrified to find that the brilliant young pianist who could cope with any technical problem of modern music did not know any of the Beethoven trios. Where in his early youth in Berlin André had learnt the Beethoven symphonies in duet form with his father, and had heard and played sonatas in his father's chamber-music recitals at home, the repertory of piano trios and quartets had been a little beyond his father's technical range, and so he had never got to know them. Szigeti's response was immediate. He proposed a weekly meeting every Monday, and so it happened for months on end that André with Szigeti and Vandenburg played through the whole classical repertory of piano trios, all the Beethovens, the Brahms, the Schuberts, the Mozarts in intensive sessions: supper followed by two hours of playing, coffee or a drink and two hours more. It was another plank in a musical education that has few parallels in its breadth of experience.

André was 18 when in 1948 he was asked to do a film score of his own. Robert Sisk, a distinguished producer who had been connected with the Theatre Guild in New York, asked him to do the score for a screenplay by Marjorie Kinnan Rawlings, authoress of *The Yearling* and winner of the Pulitzer Prize. It was called *The Sun Comes Up*, and from the quality of the screen-play Previn concludes that she must have been "drunk with money" when she wrote it. The cast—in order of billing—was Lassie, Jeanette Macdonald and Lloyd Nolan, Miss Macdonald singing for the last time on the screen. "It was a wonderful film for me," Previn comments, "because almost no one spoke. A lot of barking, an occasional song, endless scenery and the background music never stopped." André wrote "reams of descriptive music", a whole sixty minutes of it, of which he was very proud at the time, but which he prefers not to think about too closely now. The following year he was again asked to do a score of his own for a police melodrama called *Scene of the Crime* starring Van Johnson. This time the producer was a relative of Louis B. Mayer's, who promptly told his young composer that he wanted to use as a theme the Mexican folk-tune *Cielito Lindo*. That request puzzled André, who went back to ask his boss why, thinking there must be symbolical reasons. "Because it's my favourite song", came the pat answer.

One vital development took place as a result of Previn's promotion to being a fully-billed film composer: he conducted the MGM Orchestra in his own scores. The story is told round Hollywood that when the 18-year-old came up on the podium for the first time before the sixty distinguished members of the orchestra, the top instrumentalists in the profession most of whom had graduated from America's biggest orchestras, all of them much older than him, he was subjected to a harsh test. He asked for an A from the oboe, and the musician gave him an A flat, to which the rest of the orchestra, confident of showing the youngster up, immediately tuned. Previn let them do it, but as he raised his baton, he said brightly: "Right, everybody transpose a half-tone up".

He had already conducted the California Youth Symphony a number of times for Peter Meremblum, so that he was not a complete tiro, but he still thinks his cheek was formidable, knowing "damned near nothing". What helped to save him was that the players knew him as the fellow who answered questions when the nominal 'ghost' composers were faced with any sort of problem from the orchestra. They appreciated that he had actually written the scores, knew their difficulties and knew how to transpose—a basic skill unknown to many a Hollywood composer. They were therefore much more kindly disposed to him than to those who had stepped into jobs for non-musical reasons. "All I know," Previn says, "is that through their kindness I got away with it. Then as soon as I had conducted for two days I realised that it was all I ever wanted to do. It was an instant and complete revelation."

CONDUCTING, THE ARMY AND JAZZ

Though it took another twelve years before André Previn set about becoming a serious conductor full-time, it was not just in the film studios, recording his own scores, that he developed his conducting technique. Not many aspiring conductors are presented with such a happy situation as Previn was. He discovered that the players—many of whom had come from Toscanini's NBC Orchestra—were not completely satisfied playing the ephemeral music which accompanied most films. It brought them salaries considerably bigger than those of players in symphony orchestras outside, but they still hankered after playing music they could genuinely respect. So it was that three or four rehearsal orchestras were formed which would meet in high schools and civic halls simply for the pleasure of it to play through the standard repertory.

As soon as Previn let it be known that he would like to conduct them, he was given every opportunity. They would tell him they wanted to play Brahms's Second Symphony or Beethoven's Pastoral, and he would prepare it. "I would do them frightfully badly, but I would do them without an audience and learn." The actual complement of players was as often as not extraordinarily ill-balanced. "You never knew who was working that night, so that you might end up with six flutes but only one clarinet, but those seven players would be sensational. There was always something we could play."

In the studio Previn's conducting technique developed rapidly. "The main trick," he says, "was knowing what was on the paper, and being able to explain it. The other trick was a technical point for which fortunately I had a gift: I had a built-in stop-watch in my head, and it never bothered me to hit cues to the second." Anyone who has ever seen a film score being recorded, with the players sitting below a screen showing the particular film sequence will realise that this 'gift' is something which usually has to be worked at very hard by the conductor in charge.

After *Scene of the Crime* he went on to write a sequence of scores of his own, his billing gradually getting more substantial until he was promoted to a feature musical starring Vera-Ellen, called *Three Little Words*. Then came the upset. He was drafted into the American army. It was the time of the Korean War, he was just 20, and he recalls with black-humoured vividness the shock of his translation from Hollywood and its glamour to a cheerless training camp near the Canadian border. "One day I was being given a farewell lunch at MGM with composers in velour shirts and weeping nubile starlets, and then at 4 am the next morning I found myself by the tracks in the freight yard ready to be shipped off."

It was an unusually cold winter, Previn remembers, and Washington State near the Canadian border is not the most comfortable place at such a time. It did not help that the major-general commanding the division with which he was training for the US infantry hated the idea of 'showbiz' and its personalities, and he was determined that Private Previn was not going to have an easy time simply on account of his reputation as a film composer and jazz pianist. Quite the opposite. Previn remembers that he was digging a latrine trench, when an orderly came running out to tell him that he had been nominated for an Academy Award on the strength of *Three Little Words*. He remembers too that on New Year's Eve he was put on guard duty. "I was standing in this steadily falling snow, and I heard the bells tolling midnight, and there I was, absolutely awash with self-pity. At that moment one of the dogs which always hangs around army camps looking for rubbish came up, and I was so pleased to see anything that moved that

I actually said out loud to the dog: 'Happy New Year!' And he bit me."
Private Previn had to be taken off guard to have his wounded leg dressed.

Despite the major-general and his determination that Previn was not going to do anything easy, word came through from Washington DC that he should be offered a teaching job at the army music school in the capital. With it would come the rank of First Lieutenant, and Previn had visions of living off base in a civilised city. It was tempting. The snag was that he would have to sign on for four years in the army instead of merely two as a conscript. "I picked two, and it didn't go down very well."

Even so in his second year he found himself a comfortable niche. He had decided fairly early on that it was useless to fight the system. "If I was going to be there, I wasn't out to win medals, but I might as well do it as well as I could," he says, and within a year he had become a sergeant. It was as a sergeant that he went down to San Francisco to the headquarters of the Sixth Army attached to special services. There he was told to work with the Sixth Army band as concertmaster. It was quite a good band, he remembers, and characteristically to relieve the inevitable boredom of arranging regular military band music, "I finally did really crazy things that seem wildly eccentric, like arranging Shostakovich's First Symphony for band."

Previn stayed in San Francisco for the last six months of his two-year stint in the Army, and it was during that time that Pierre Monteux, then principal conductor of the San Francisco Symphony, agreed to take him on as one of his conducting pupils. Monteux, he remembers, had no idea of army authority. At one of his lessons Previn told Monteux that his name was on the next draft to Japan, which at the time almost certainly meant an assignment to the front in Korea. When Monteux heard that his pupil was going to Tokyo, his response was that the Tokyo Philharmonic was not in his view as good as it had been cracked up to be, and that Previn should tell the army that it was not worth his going there.

It was at this time that Leonard Bernstein made his first appearance as a conductor on the West Coast with the Israel Philharmonic Orchestra. Previn went to the Friday night concert in San Francisco and was completely bowled over. "It was the key to the absolute. If you think that Lennie's active now, he really used to dance up a storm in those days—a fabulous concert." On the Saturday and Sunday too the adoring Previn managed to follow Bernstein to his concerts at Berkeley and Stanford, and then on Monday came his next lesson with Monteux. He was told to take the orchestra in the opening of Brahms's Fourth Symphony, but after only thirty seconds came hand-clapping from the hall. Monteux beckoned Previn back to him so that he could speak without the others hearing. Previn leaned over. "You went to see Mr Bernstein?" Monteux asked knowingly. "Go back and do it again!" Then after the rehearsal, when the lesson was well and truly learnt by the pupil, Monteux put his arm round Previn and said: "Dear boy, before you try to impress the ladies in the mezzanine, make sure the horns come in!"

When he was released from the Army Previn decided not to go back to

Opposite: Touché! [EMI/Clive Barda

28

Hollywood immediately. He felt he was not ready to return, and he deliberately deceived his film employers so that he could stay for a time in San Francisco. "I lived in a terrible single room above somebody's garage at the back of the house with linoleum on the floor and an outside loo. I stayed up there on those strange buckling floors figuring out how to make sandwiches. I didn't even know how to do that. But I was studying and having a good time." He was fortunate in being able to keep the wolf from the door by doing the occasional orchestration for the live variety shows on radio and the cabarets presented on the Fairmount and Mark Hopkins Hotels. It was almost like Las Vegas, he remembers, with all the most successful night-club acts appearing, Lena Horne and so on. "They would pay me 25 dollars for an arrangement which should have been 200 dollars, and that kept me going when I was too broke to go to the market. I still have a great affection for San Francisco. If you can be dead broke in a city and still love it, then it speaks very well for it."

Previn stayed a year in San Francisco after getting out of the army. One of his main reasons was to continue his lessons with Pierre Monteux. He now already had in mind the ambition to become a serious conductor, but other things "got in the way", even before he returned to Hollywood and the MGM music department. It was in San Francisco that he met his first wife, Betty Bennett, "who was and is an absolutely first-rate jazz-singer". She introduced André to the jazz world of San Francisco, and he became more and more interested in jazz outside the popular commercial vein which he had been exploiting till then. As he says, he now came upon "a more rarefied sphere of jazz", and he was fascinated.

After a year he had for family reasons to return to Los Angeles, but like others who had had a couple of years away in the forces he could not face going back to the family home, and being—at least to a degree—supervised once more by his parents. The result was predictable. "Suddenly here was Betty, and she was pretty, and we were fond of each other, and we shared this enthusiasm for jazz, and we got married." The couple set up home in Hollywood, and André returned to the MGM studio, to take up his career where he left off. His four years of marriage with Betty, he explains, were the highspot of his jazz career. Betty introduced him in Los Angeles, as she had done in San Francisco, to a whole range of jazz musicians with less commercial but musically more interesting ideas. He could afford not to take a strong commercial line because never in his career was Previn a full-time jazz musician. His jazz piano playing was always a side-line, and it never took more than a fairly small fraction of his time. It was at this period, when as he puts it "I became serious about jazz as I became serious about all music", that he started recording for Contemporary, a less commercially-minded—and much smaller—company than RCA.

The label was run by an individualist called Lester Koenig, who in 1954 suggested that Previn should make a record with his jazz colleagues, Shelly Manne and Leroy Vinnegar. They turned up at a converted warehouse which Koenig used as a studio, and the idea was to work all night. At first they could not make up their minds what to play. The current hit on Broadway at the time was *My Fair Lady*, and Koenig suggested jazz versions of the whole score to make up an album. But then they found that none of them knew more than the two hit numbers, *On the street where you live* and *I'm just accustomed to your face*. What happened was that they sent out to an all-night record store and got a copy of the original cast recording. They listened to one track at a time, and roughly figured out what they wanted to do. Then they would record that particular track. By dawn they had completed the album.

It is a familiar feature of Previn's career that some project entered into with fair innocence, with no special concern for its commercial success, should blow up unexpectedly. When the album was finished, Koenig became worried that the original composers, Lerner and Loewe, might object at what some might consider a parody. In the end they described it as 'a piano version', but they need not have worried, for Lerner and Loewe were delighted with it. At the time it was the biggest-selling jazz disc that the record industry had ever known, and its success—selling roughly half a million LPs—was almost an embarrassment to a tiny record company which till then did not even have a shipping office, and which boasted a proprietor who with his wife and friends crated the records himself and sent them off.

After that there was a formula to exploit, and the three friends did a whole series of similar records based on shows, but only one of the others— based on Bernstein's *West Side Story*—does Previn really approve of today. In that the melodies were unusual enough in the first place and warranted unusual treatment. As for *My Fair Lady*, he feels that it was certainly adventurous when it came out, but it became too ready a formula, easily copied, not just by himself and his colleagues. Those who have compared the sleeves of the discs which Previn did at this time with Shelly Manne and Leroy Vinnegar may have wondered about the shuffling about of the leadership— André Previn and his pals, Shelly Manne and his friends, and so on. "It was a real jazz musicians' reasoning, no question of rivalry." The leader of the group in any session got an initial $200 against the $100 each for the other two. It "didn't matter a damn who was leader", so they took it in turns, and shared the royalties evenly too. "The nice thing about jazz musicians is that there is very little jockeying for position."

Of his other jazz records the ones Previn still likes make a comparatively short list. He mentions first a disc called *4 to Go* in which he was joined by Ray Brown on the bass, Shelly Manne on the drums and Herbie Ellis on the guitar. Then there was a disc of *The Theatre Songs of Kurt Weill* which he did with J. J. Johnson, "a phenomenal trombone player". It was a critical success, he reports, but did not sell well. He also confesses an affection for a disc he did for RCA, *André Previn, All alone*. It consisted of jazz piano versions of well-known 'standards'. The idea was for him to go to the studio, and there thumb through a random pile of sheet music. He would sit down and do an improvisation of any tune that hit him. Each time he did a single improvisation, and never attempted a second take of anything. The result was that after three hours they had twenty-two numbers recorded, twelve of which they selected for the finished *All alone* disc. "I like some of them, because they are so obviously improvisatory", Previn comments.

Returning to the MGM studio after army service and his time in San Francisco presented fewer problems than one might expect. Though the movie business has always been keenly competitive, it was a time in the early 'fifties when so many films were being made that Previn was able very easily to slot back into the role he had established for himself before he left. "I had been good at what I was doing", he comments, "and from MGM's point of view I hadn't been all that expensive. They were pleased to see me back." He was fortunate that Arthur Freed, producer of MGM's biggest musicals at the time, took a liking to him, and quickly he was given prime place among the composers for musical spectaculars. The pattern was for him to do an original score as opposed to an arrangement of a stage show every third film. He preferred it that way, finding it all great fun, but even so he says, "there are very few of my scores I can listen to now with equanimity". Curiously, he notes, the combination of a good score and a good film did not come to him very often. Some scores he does like were for films that were far from good, and he instances above all his favourite among his film-scores which "I wrote for the worst film I was ever connected with, *The Four Horsemen of the Apocalypse*. It was hilariously bad. They wanted an endless score for an enormous orchestra and they gave me a lot of time. It was originally a four-hour picture, and they cut two full hours out of it after the director left, so that scenes and dialogue were alluded to that the audience had never seen. There was a huge dramatic moment with a shatteringly explosive passage from me where the hero and heroine were on the Pont Neuf in Paris. She whirled on him, and said: 'Then take your *key* back!', and of course no one had ever seen that he'd given her a key in the first place. And while I went berserk in the orchestra, screaming around, people in the audience kept whispering: 'What key? What key?' It was a dismal failure." At least Previn feels that his apocalyptic score was reasonably imaginative musically.

Of his other films Previn lists *Elmer Gantry*, *Bad Day at Black Rock* and *Inside Daisy Clover* as the ones he still likes. Nowadays he tends to cringe when old movies appear on television, and the BBC's arrangement with MGM means that they come along frequently in Britain.

A typical Previn musical of the period was *It's always fair weather* of 1955, starring Gene Kelly, Dan Dailey and Michael Kidd as three friends demobbed from the army, who agree to meet up in ten years time in a particular bar. Whether or not Previn, himself demobbed not so long before, felt particular identification with the plot, his score includes two long virtuoso passages taking up practically the first half-hour of the film—more or less a military version of what Bernstein had done for his three sailors in *On the Town*. The variations on the main theme may not be particularly original—one could hardly distinguish the writing from many other scores of the genre— but the ingenuity with which Previn switches from one idea to another is

Opposite.
Above left: Alicia Previn, aged 10.

Above right: Claudia Previn, aged 12.

Below: With Alicia, 1971.
[EMI/David Farrell

characteristically brilliant, providing a musical equivalent of swift montage. Plainly he had no lack whatever of musical ideas appropriate to his purpose, even when, as in the first of several scenes of drunken revelry he sets off with a clarinet theme and chromatic parallel chords that present a straight crib from Gershwin's *Rhapsody in Blue*. But cribbing was a necessary part of writing such a score in order to please the customer in a predictable way. Previn was exceptionally adept at providing a Cole Porter style number where necessary, a parody of a high school song, or best of all a genuine sweet, sentimental number with a first-rate tune, *When the time has come for parting*, used liberally through the film but not plugged "eighty times over" in the way that, as he complains, has become too prevalent in later movies.

Only once in his career as a staff composer for MGM was Previn put on suspension for refusing to carry out a commission. That was when he was told to work with the tenor, Mario Lanza, someone whom he found "as offensive as he was untalented". Previn thought it no way to spend six months writing a film for him, and he went happily on suspension, noting all those composers who had gone white-haired working alongside the tenor. "But three days later," he explains, "they wanted me badly to do another picture, so my heroic stand was minuscule."

Almost every year during this period he was nominated for an Oscar, an Academy Award, for the best film score of the year. The first had been *Three Little Words* just as he went in the army, and from then on in fourteen years he was nominated ten times. But ironically he won only one Oscar while he was still on the MGM staff, and that was for *Gigi* in 1958, a Lerner and Loewe musical, which incidentally also inspired one of his jazz improvisation discs with Shelly Manne and Leroy Vinnegar. After that he decided to take his chance as a free-lance, hired for individual films at a much greater fee. This move towards independence was, as it proved, a step towards serious music, but it could easily have been otherwise.

While his career both in films and as a jazz pianist had been prospering, his marriage with Betty Bennett had foundered. "We were married much too early", he says today. "We weren't mature enough to cope. Though we shared our enthusiasm for jazz, we didn't in the long run have all that much to share. When we meet nowadays we really are close friends, and I like to think my daughters, Claudia and Alicia, love me genuinely as a father. Alicia has just stayed with me here in England for two years, till she got homesick for California and Claudia visited us here too. Now when I see Betty we get on so well that I wonder if with hindsight we could have been smart enough to have a totally different marriage. As it was, it was hopeless."

They were divorced after four years. Betty Bennett has never married again, and remains a highly successful jazz singer. It was during his first marriage that Previn's jazz career reached its peak, and then in reaction the break-up of his marriage helped to encourage once more his ambitions in the classical field. He directed the rehearsal orchestras of studio players with great enjoyment—the more so as a result of his lessons with Monteux—but he was still better known as a pianist rather than as a conductor.

His classical ambitions were vigorously encouraged when he met his second wife, Dory. Her ambition was to be a serious writer and poet, and was trying to earn a living as a writer of lyrics for songs. Arthur Freed, the MGM musical producer, had noted her in New York, brought her to Hollywood to work with Previn, but somehow forgot to tell him. So it was, at a time when he was working on three films simultaneously and was incessantly busy to the point of impatience, "this very attractive young woman would leap at me with lyrics, and say 'Whenever you want to look at these, Mr Previn'. I finally said 'Arthur, who the hell is that girl?' Freed replied 'My God, that's your collaborator. I forgot to tell you'." That, Previn notes, was typical of Hollywood, and by a strange irony when he was free to work with Dory on a later picture (for he had found her lyrics not merely good but brilliant) her option had been dropped by the studio.

Their subsequent professional collaboration was not on whole films but on individual tunes. "Some of them were very good, and some even quite successful. All of them had a quality I was pleased with." He recorded some with Leontyne Price and Eileen Farrell.

It was some time after they had collaborated professionally, that the relationship became personal. Previn, by now tired once more of bachelor freedom, married Dory, and found a helpmate who urged him positively to take the difficult step of turning his back on a brilliantly successful career writing film music, and taking the decidedly risky course of becoming a conductor.

THE NEW CAREER

After Previn left the staff of MGM in 1958, he was even more successful than previously. As a freelance he went on to win three more Oscars in the following years—*Porgy and Bess*, in 1959; *Irma la Douce*, in 1963 and *My Fair Lady*, in 1964. But long before 1964 the firm decision had been taken that he would leave his career in films behind. "Round the age of thirty I looked at myself in the mirror, and said, 'Let's face it: you're wasting your time'."

He had already established a reputation as a classical pianist. With Israel Baker and Edgar Lustgarten he formed the Pacific Arts Trio, and together they gave something like a hundred concerts, basically for pleasure. At the University of California, Los Angeles, with members of the Roth Quartet he also gave annual cycles of the Beethoven Trios. Later he came to play concertos—Prokofiev's Third, Rachmaninov's *Paganini Rhapsody*, Beethoven's Third and *Emperor*, a number of Mozart works—with orchestras of the calibre of the Boston Symphony and the New York Philharmonic. An encounter which Previn had with the redoubtable George Szell in a Los Angeles hotel brought characteristic flashes from both of them. Did Previn know the Strauss *Burleske*, Szell asked? Previn replied that he did (a rare work), whereupon Szell asked him to play the opening bars. Previn in astonishment looked round for a piano, and Szell rather testily told him to play on the edge of the table. Feeling rather a fool, Previn obeyed, only to have Szell

snap out: "Too slow, too slow!" But Previn was not to be cowed. "I'm afraid I'm used to tables with quicker action", he fired back. Szell promptly let it be known he did not think the remark funny. "Well I do", said Previn, and left. He did not play in Cleveland.

Conducting proved a more difficult problem. Like other Hollywood musicians before him with similarly serious ambitions, he had a series of dilemmas to face. Fortunately two highly influential figures in the music world provided the necessary spur just at the moment when he needed it. One of Previn's concerts with a rehearsal orchestra in a school auditorium was attended by chance by Schuyler Chapin, at one time of CBS, more recently at the Met, and by Ronald Wilford, Vice-President of Columbia Artists, the big American music management firm. It was they, deeply impressed, who suggested to Previn that rather than going on as a part-time classical pianist (an overcrowded profession, they thought) he should turn to conducting. They could hardly have suspected in making this suggestion they were tapping one of Previn's most cherished—if dormant—ambitions. They did not disguise the fact that it would involve a big loss of income (to this day Previn has still not equalled his highest figures as a film composer) and would mean a great deal of tiresome travelling. Previn's response was prompt, but even after the main decision was taken with the enthusiastic encouragement of Dory, he allowed that it would be wise to continue doing just one film score a year in case he had to return, tail between his legs, to "the not entirely unpleasant business of scoring films".

The first offers for Previn's services as a conductor, some as early as 1954, came from the most distinguished orchestras—from Philadelphia, New York, Cleveland, Chicago and Boston. But all these offers were for Previn as a conductor of popular music. They wanted Cole Porter nights, Rodgers and Hammerstein nights, Gershwin nights, and Previn realised very clearly that in essence that was exactly what he was doing already, and did not have to leave home to do it. The offers were seductive, and they were of the kind that other Hollywood men had readily accepted, but Previn's ambitions were different. In a way his decision to turn down these offers, which redoubled when it was known he wanted to become a conductor, was more courageous than his initial decision to make the change. He could have argued to himself that the pop nights might lead to more serious engagements, but instead he insisted that any conducting dates from the start should be for serious programmes, for the regular repertory from Haydn to Britten.

Understanding as he was, Ronald Wilford, by now Previn's agent, pointed out that he could arrange a conducting tour for him using such serious repertory, but "the biggest city will be Kalamazoo". Previn agreed. He does not disguise the fact that he started with two distinct advantages over direct rivals setting out on a conducting career. In the first place his years of affluence had left him with a sound financial base, if hardly a great store of wealth. In the second his name was known. He likes to suggest that on his first conducting tours to semi-professional orchestras in various towns throughout the United States—often on a fee little more than his plane-fare—

the audiences would come simply because of his name, and would then groan when they saw he was performing Haydn instead of Gershwin and would not even touch the keyboard. What was certainly true was that a high proportion of the reviews after these concerts began with the description "Hollywood's André Previn . . . ", and proceeded at best to patronise him, but more frequently to damn him simply through his association with the despised film world.

It was an attitude that took a long time to break, but Previn's early successes were sufficiently encouraging for him to push on relentlessly. When he returned for another concert and another after that to any one place, the journalistic peg had as a rule to be modified, and finally even in the press he felt he was coming to be accepted for his own musical qualities as a conductor and not for any outside associations. "I worked hard", he explains. "The orchestras got better, the engagements got bigger, and then I was able to do the big orchestras." It helped in every engagement right from the start that his rehearsal technique was so crisply efficient. One thing that Hollywood had taught him relentlessly was not to waste time, and he would use every minute of a rehearsal to the best effect, where many fine conductors—and many not so fine—behave as though they have all the time in the world.

The schedule was tough. Ronald Wilford, like the enthusiastic manager he was, pushed in every possible engagement. As Previn says: "He tended to look at prospective dates and merely ask 'Can the plane make it?'" Managers, he feels, forget what has to go on between every concert, not merely the rehearsing but the mechanics of picking life up and putting it down in different places daily. At one point Previn, exasperated, persuaded Wilford to come along with him for a week to see what it was like. After seven days the manager was worn to a shred and promised without prompting that he would never make André take midnight planes again. This, Previn admits, was not quite a fair test, since he himself had his music-making to think of, a keen purpose from concert to concert to help keep him going, and that was less tiring than merely observing as a comparatively unoccupied companion. They did a test once, Previn remembers, on a young, tough American football player, who was asked to stand up on a platform for the length of a symphony and wave his arms. He did not manage it, for unlike a conductor—whether an octogenarian or not—he had nothing to distract him from the sheer effort he was making.

In this process Previn matured as a conductor. His training had been long and detailed—disguised as it was by the dozens of other activities which kept him in the public eye—but it was the actual experience of working through the regular repertory with symphony orchestras at live concerts, not just the eager players of the Hollywood rehearsal orchestras but less skilled, more cynical musicians in the backwoods orchestras and their amateur colleagues, which developed his understanding. He remembers a performance of Brahms's First Symphony that he gave during this period. On the day of the performance he had been deeply upset by personal news that had come to him. "As a result I went out on stage," he says, "and I poured all my feelings into the performance. I became totally immersed in the music, and at the end of it I thought I had given a really superb performance, certainly the best of which I was then capable. I came off into the wings, and there was Ronald Wilford. He said: 'What the hell was that just now? That was the most tasteless wallowing around I ever heard'. I was furious. I could hardly speak to him. Luckily that performance had been taped, and the next morning I listened to it. It *was* the most tasteless wallowing around I had ever heard."

There you have a characteristic example of Previn's ability to learn from experience, his genuine power to take note not only of his own mistakes but of the responses of others. His determination not to be a mandarin may disconcert some who look for dictatorial conductors wearing big cloaks of self-importance, but there is little doubt that his responsiveness makes for communication of an intensity that audiences everywhere at once recognise. This was the development of his own innate talents which in the field of conducting emerged from his period of comparatively unglamorous touring. He was ready to emerge on the world stage.

It is sad that Previn's father never lived to see the fulfilment of his son's promise in a role which he himself would have applauded. Jack Previn remained completely unimpressed through the years by any of André's popular successes. He never accused his son of prostituting his art, but he was sufficiently out of sympathy with jazz to regard André's jazz piano work as unimportant ("It is not the 'Eroica'," was his very German comment on ephemeral music). As for André's film work, it was something which he regarded as essentially trivial, and even the award of an Oscar—a milestone which André did reach before his father died—left him cold. He was pleased for André's sake, but it was not the fulfilment for which he had always looked. Particularly after his arrival in America when his own brilliant career as a lawyer was destroyed, and he had to turn in makeshift to teaching children to play the piano, he lived—as Steve Previn says—for André's success. He knew that his son had the ingredients in him to be an outstanding musician in the world of classical music, where he himself had attempted to lead him. His instinct was sure, but he died just as André was turning his own difficult corner, just before acclaim started to come in the field of serious conducting.

Jack Previn's death in 1963 came four years after the death of his only daughter, Leonore, still in her twenties. It is significant that the doctors, once they had diagnosed cancer, told not the parents but the younger son, André. Steve Previn was in Europe at the time. André rang him in Vienna, and he returned. He was never sure whether he was right in keeping the news of Leonore's illness from his parents until the last minute. On the death of his daughter, Jack Previn seemed according to his son to become overnight an old man. When he died four years later, André had the job of making the funeral arrangements. Deeply upset as he was, he was not a person to linger regretfully. At Forest Lawn, the huge cemetery in Los Angeles, he refused to be badgered into funereal ostentation. He talks today of the experience with a characteristic mixture of emotion and black humour.

His own private life was made more difficult by the problems of his marriage to Dory. She was vital in encouraging him in his conducting career, but she herself desperately searched for success of her own. It was not enough for her merely to reflect her husband's career. She wanted to be a writer and poet, and Previn today finds it "ironic but very fair that the minute we split up, she became a great success". He is genuinely delighted that latterly her work as a pop writer and performer has found its fulfilment.

During their marriage one of the problems lay in her unavoidable reluctance to travel. His tours as a conductor often took him away from their home in Los Angeles for months on end, almost always for the greater part of the year, and in the end it was no real marriage for either of them. She herself since the divorce has made public her own mental problems, her recurrent attacks of illness, which darkened any relationship. It was a great trouble to them both, which at the time they could not share with the outside world.

In his professional career as a conductor the turning point for Previn came with his arrival as a recording artist, and more specifically with his first collaboration with the London Symphony Orchestra. It is no exaggeration to say that Previn's international reputation as a conductor could never have developed rapidly as it did, had he not had the chance to make records. With his recorded performances there came the opportunity of being judged by less biased critics—professional writers and the public at large—in a way that reflected on his positive qualities. Those who had hardly heard of his Hollywood work were able to disregard the unwanted associations and judge on merit.

In becoming an important recording conductor, Previn was helped, as so often before, by his experience in those ephemeral media. His ability to rehearse an orchestra and not waste a second of the players' time, to understand their problems from the inside, had been established in his film work and applied to serious interpretation over his apprenticeship on the unglamorous orchestral circuit, but it was equally important that his film work involved recording, getting a performance "into the can" so that the end result would sound spontaneous. Alongside such recording for the studios, there was from the time he was 16 his recording work for RCA and others as a jazz pianist. That too taught him very clearly how live qualities could best be conveyed in disc form. His recording career on the classical side also involved playing the piano. For Columbia records in America he made a number of LPs of solo piano music covering "repertory that was not exactly fought over by others"—Hindemith, Frank Martin, Barber, Copland, Roussel and Poulenc. He also made records of chamber music—the Fauré and Mendelssohn Trios, the Toch Piano Quintet and Chausson's Piano Quartet. But from the record company's point of view this was all extremely esoteric music, and none of his records sold.

By this time he had begun to conduct the more successful orchestras outside the top six in America—St Louis Symphony, Los Angeles Philharmonic, Pittsburgh Symphony—and to his delight Columbia Records asked him to make his first serious record as a conductor. With the St Louis Symphony Orchestra he recorded a coupling of Britten's *Sinfonia da Requiem* and Copland's *The Red Pony*. "They worked very hard, and they were good to me, but the playing is just not terribly great." Though considering the limitations the result was a great success, the record company made it clear that with Bruno Walter, George Szell, Leonard Bernstein, Eugene Ormandy, not to mention Aaron Copland and Igor Stravinsky on their roster there was not going to be all that much space for André Previn as a conductor, particularly not when another young hopeful Thomas Schippers was recording for them too.

It took some years to arrange, but the end result was that Previn asked CBS to release him from his contract—which they were perfectly willing to do provided he did not make the same kind of pop records for rivals as he had for them. It was Roger Hall of RCA who then in October 1964— eighteen months having elapsed after the Britten/Copland record—arranged for Previn to go to London to record concerto accompaniments with the Royal Philharmonic Orchestra. Two of these were with Lorin Hollander— the Khachaturian Piano Concerto and Bloch's *Scherzo Fantasque*—and two were with Leonard Pennario—the First and Fourth Piano Concertos of Rachmaninov. As a pianist himself, perfectly capable of performing any of these works at the keyboard in his own right, Previn demonstrated at once his unusual sympathy as a concerto conductor, no rival at all, rather an understander.

Recording Brahms, August 1972.
[Edward Greenfield

The result was that though the finished discs had limited commercial success, Previn was at once asked to do two records of symphonies with the London Symphony Orchestra. Here at last was the chance he needed. In August 1965 he went over to London again, and there at Walthamstow Assembly Rooms he recorded Shostakovich's Fifth Symphony and Tchaikovsky's Second with Liadov's Eight Russian Folksongs for coupling in sessions that proved the start of a love affair. The members of the LSO, the keenest professionals to their fingertips, were charmed by a conductor who initially they had suspected was being foisted on them merely on account of his name in the pop world. Quickly RCA, observing the startling success of the collaboration, signed up Previn and the LSO to do a whole series of sessions at intervals of only a few months—Rachmaninov's Second Symphony in April 1966, Walton's First Symphony in August of that year, Nielsen's First in February 1967, and a series of no fewer than four discs in the summer of that year.

One of the four—made with the English Chamber Orchestra, Previn's only non-LSO record after the love affair started—was of Mozart's brief comic opera *The Impresario*, and this brought a new text and new play by Dory Previn. André's marriage was already strained, but he took the opportunity of promoting his wife's professional interests as well as his own.

More important in the long run were the signs of Previn's long-held allegiance to British music. From his schooldays in California he had found the closest affinity with the music of Walton and Vaughan Williams in particular. Walton's jazz inflections came very close to Previn's own mode of expression, and it was significant that when he recorded Walton's First Symphony he had to face direct competition with one of Walton's longest-established interpreters, Sir Malcolm Sargent, whose version of the Symphony with the New Philharmonia Orchestra for HMV appeared in the same month as Previn's on RCA. The acclaim for Previn even over the veteran Waltonian was universal. It was plain that here was an important new interpretative voice.

Previn's Anglophilia was cemented by London itself and the English countryside. Over his years of travelling he found regularly that where normally on arriving in a new city, his initial reaction was "Well here we go again", his response to London even at the less-than-beautiful sight of Heathrow Airport was to say "Thank goodness". He felt at home, and even now, an established British resident who has learned most of the snags of life in England, he insists he will never take the feel of the country for granted, its physical impact.

Previn's recording sessions with the LSO led as soon as was practicable to concert dates with the orchestra at the Royal Festival Hall and elsewhere. Those confirmed with the self-governing members of the orchestra the powers of a conductor who was extraordinarily quick in establishing his box-office appeal with the British public. It was before one of these concerts, a performance of Liszt's rarely heard *Faust* Symphony, that in the Savoy Hotel, where he was staying, he bumped into someone he had known for some years, the actress Mia Farrow. Her marriage with Frank Sinatra had already failed. He told her he was conducting that night, and invited her to the concert. She confessed that she had never been to an orchestral concert in her life before, and said she would be delighted to come. As Previn that night raised his baton to direct an unusually thorny work, one not readily appreciated even by experienced music-lovers, he thought: "Poor girl! What a thing to do to her."

PRINCIPAL CONDUCTOR

Previn's peak of activity in the recording studio with the LSO in the summer of 1967—among other things setting out on the long haul of a complete cycle of Vaughan Williams symphonies—was followed immediately by his arrival in Houston as Musical Director of the Houston Symphony Orchestra. It was his first permanent conducting post, and an important step forward, because this orchestra, pride of a relentless oil city that determinedly mixes culture with its money-making, had had as its previous musical directors figures no less venerable than Leopold Stokowski and Sir John Barbirolli. Barbirolli had managed over a number of seasons to combine his post in Houston with that of principal conductor of the Hallé Orchestra in Manchester, and with the opening of a fine new hall in Houston in 1966 the reputation of the orchestra had never stood higher.

The fact that Previn was asked to be musical director—still considered as a

largely untried figure—reflected the orchestra's enjoyment of earlier engagements with him. From the start he worked hard to consolidate the orchestra.
Soon after his appointment he found that the orchestra's principal cellist,
Shirley Trepel, an artist whose work Previn admired enormously, was being
wooed away from Houston by an offer from the Cleveland Orchestra.
Promptly he promised her that he would write a cello concerto for her to
play in Houston the following season, if only she would stay. He kept his
word. That summer he wrote the concerto, one of his most important works.

His Houston itinerary was taxing, for it included not only the concert
series on home ground in Houston itself, but concert tours "of the kind that
can only be devised in the southern part of the United States". They involved
playing in the most unsuitable halls—university and high school gymnasiums
often enough where the only dressing accommodation was the football
team's locker room. There would be no proscenium and no stage lights,
and they would be staying in hotels which Previn felt were not good enough
for a fine orchestra. On one day he remembers resolving to himself before a
concert which could readily have been left off the itinerary that he would
simply beat his way through Schubert's *Great* C major Symphony and not
try to convey its emotional message. That was all the place was worth, he
felt. But, as he confesses, after a mere 16 bars his intention was completely
forgotten. "I couldn't get away with it, because in essence I was really
double-crossing Schubert. That piece was certainly better than any performance could ever convey. I pulled myself together, made my change of
feelings known to the orchestra—just as disgruntled as I was—and it did
end up being a credibly fervent performance. Whether any of it got over

Top: Previn and the LSO
rehearse in Wells Cathedral.
[Mary Lawrence

Above: Previn, newly chosen as
principal conductor of the LSO,
with Harold Lawrence, the
orchestra's General Manager.
[Mary Lawrence

43

the vast expanse of the basket-ball court I don't know, but by Christ we were trying."

Even as he tells you of such an experience, Previn reveals his own continuing fervour. He regarded his appointment to Houston as an important milestone in his career, but it was nothing to the milestone which came next. It was about this time in London that he took part in the BBC's longest-running radio programme, *Desert Island Discs*, and as usual at the end, after Previn had given his choices of record which he would take if cast away on a desert island, Roy Plomley, the interviewer, asked him of his further ambitions. He admitted that it was presumptuous of him, but his aim beyond any other was to become principal conductor of the orchestra with which he had always felt he had a special relationship, the LSO. By a strange trick of fate six months later he was offered that very post. The LSO had come to an amicable agreement with Istvan Kertesz, its previous principal conductor, to end the contract, and the choice of successor of the members and their board of directors was André Previn.

The first problem was that like Kertesz before him, Previn now had other important commitments outside England. It would be impossible for him to cancel most of the engagements he had for example with his other orchestra in Houston, but there was no doubt whatever in Previn's mind that once the offer was made from the LSO he had to find some means of fitting in all the necessary commitments. For more than a year he kept his promise to the Houston Symphony that his new post would not interfere with any of his concerts in Texas. It meant commuting from London to Houston with formidable frequency. "I think the airlines owe me some kind of medal."

Even so there was hardly any let-up in his recording schedule with the LSO, and though his contribution to the LSO's concert schedule was not as intensive as it was later to become, he still managed to conduct a quota of concerts with the orchestra over his first full season.

It was within months of his taking over as principal conductor of the LSO that Previn, always one to attract journalistic attention even without trying, found himself in the middle of the front-page gossip. He was living with Mia Farrow, and it became public knowledge that she was going to have a child. From then on, reports Previn, photographers "nested in the trees" round their London home; reporters would leap out at them as they emerged, but even this unnerving treatment failed to shake André's and Mia's Anglophilia. Both of them, long used to glaring publicity, tended to accept it as a necessary nuisance, though it intensified after Mia gave birth to two healthy boy twins, whom they named Matthew and Sascha. Both André and Mia had marital problems to sort out. On André's side he was grateful for Dory's consideration. They divided the effects of their Los Angeles home—with pictures the only significant objects of contention, both of them being devoted to modern art. Her own success in the world of popular cult figures was on the point of overtaking her.

But from the very moment when André and Mia married they ceased to be news—at least to the degree they had been enduring. They withdrew

André with Mia and her mother, Maureen O'Sullivan [David Hart

44

to a comfortable early eighteenth century house in the Vaughan Williams country near Reigate, sheltered from prying eyes by being in its own grounds. It is not large, cosy rather than ostentatious, but it has the advantage that if they put their gumboots on they can walk for a mile or so through the woods and not step off their own land. They saunter down to the local village shop— or ride on their bicycles—and within months they became an accepted part of village life, defended when necessary against outsiders. It was important to both of them, for from the start—both of them having experienced the trials of 'showbiz' marriages and their strains—they agreed that each of them needed to carry on with a separate career. The strains they understood completely in advance, whatever the gossip columns might say.

Where Mia would have to be away on film work all too often, André was still touring throughout the world. He aims to stay at home in England for roughly eight months of the year—a far bigger proportion of time than most international artists allow themselves—and in his 'away' time he does not count the tours he makes with the LSO, friends and colleagues. For three years running he went with them to the Festival at Daytona Beach, and there in unconventional but delightful surroundings he and his colleagues enjoyed themselves with almost the same easy-going abandon that he had known in his jazz days back in Hollywood with Shelly Manne, Leroy Vinnegar and the others. Following the adventurous policy of the LSO started by Ernest Fleischmann when general manager and continued by his successor, Harold Lawrence (who was already manager when Previn was appointed in 1968), the orchestra regularly made prestigious tours not only across the Atlantic but all over the world.

In the garden at home: Mia with Sascha, André with Matthew.
[David Hart

I was lucky enough to go with them on one of their longest tours to Russia and the Far East, when in exactly a month—April to May, 1971— Previn conducted a brilliant series of 18 concerts in seven cities—Moscow and Leningrad; Tokyo, Osaka and Nagoya; Seoul and Hongkong.

Observing him closely over a substantial period, I was struck even more than I expected by his energy. Mia had had to stay behind in England—at the last minute one of the twins was ill—and that added to André's tensions. He was not sleeping well. At normal times he will go for a week or so with only four or five hours a night—leaving him plenty of time for reading and studying new scores, as he explains, in compensation—but in Russia and the Far East he was managing with even less. He would regularly take a morning rehearsal involving, say, the Mozart C minor Piano Concerto, K.491, in which he himself played the solo, and he would later in the day conduct at the actual concert. In between he would be sightseeing and shopping with the rest of us, or would borrow my typewriter, and tap out a dispatch for the *New Yorker* magazine which was presenting a diary series on the tour from him. Finding it hard enough myself to get dispatches written, I marvelled at the determination to triumph over merely physical obstacles. On one day in Leningrad he even managed a session in the *Shakespeare's Sonnets* Café with the Leningrad Jazz Club, accompanying David Gray, the LSO first horn, in brilliant improvisations.

Above: Sir William Walton congratulates Previn after the LSO's performance of Walton's First Symphony in Moscow, April 1971. [Mary Lawrence

Opposite: Conducting in the Tchaikovsky Auditorium, Moscow, April 1971. [Mary Lawrence

On a similarly crowded day in Moscow we returned to the enormous *Russia* Hotel—the largest in the world, so it was claimed, housing up to 6,000 people—and knowing the rigid rules we presented ourselves together with Sir William and Lady Walton, our cherished companions on the Russian half of the trip, for some kind of meal at the not unreasonable hour of 10.30 pm, half an hour before the scheduled closing time. Previn was the only one of us who remained reasonably good-tempered through the to-ing and fro-ing of Soviet restaurant bureaucracy. When we were finally allotted our table, and Previn was looking forward to eating for the first time that day (it was one of his days coping with the Mozart concerto as well as conducting) the waiter looked angrily at us, and said firmly after all the arguments: "No food!" Led by Previn, who can see the absurdity of anything even in suffering, we sat back and laughed, deciding in the absence of food that we could at least get drunk on vodka. But as the vodka was being brought, Walton had the brilliant idea of saying in his most wrily magisterial manner: *"Käse"*, hoping that the waiter might conceivably respond to the German for cheese. And so magically he did, piling the black bread and cheese to satisfy even a famished conductor.

Considering the charisma of his stage personality, one cannot fail to be surprised that Previn refuses even under the most trying circumstances to throw his weight about. In rehearsal he is always first among equals, never a dictator, always ready to respond to advice, always ready to admit error in himself, but flashing out in a moment—no one more effective than he—on the rare occasions when anyone seeks to take advantage. His wit is of course an essential part of his technique, and though from time to time his LSO colleagues may hanker after a mandarin figure as their musical director, thumping the tub of self-importance, Previn's way of drawing out the very finest vein of their virtuosity has become more and more apparent to them over the years—to players as to audiences.

A typical moment in a Previn rehearsal came when the orchestra was on a trip to Chatham in Kent, not a vital concert but one that no one wanted to skimp. One of the items in the programme was the *Firebird Suite* of Stravinsky with its enormous horn solo, long and intense, in the final movement. It so happened that a new co-principal was playing that day. They rehearsed as far as the horn solo, and Previn closed his score to end the rehearsal. Tentatively the horn-player pointed out that he had never performed that solo before. Instead of showing any sort of concern Previn simply beamed at the player, and to hoots of delight from the rest of the orchestra, he shook his head maliciously and said: "You're going to *love* it!" Not just joking there: good technique too.

Good technique in rehearsal, wasting not a moment, goes with good technique in ordering a life that from childhood has been crammed with multifarious and often conflicting activity. In 1972, exasperated by the waste of time every morning when he would receive four or five dozen telephone calls, he actually went to the extreme of having his phone removed. As he was attached to a very small exchange there had never been much possibility of keeping his number secret from Fleet Street for long, and he steeled himself to being completely incommunicado, relenting after a few weeks to have a phone which called outwards but was inaccessible to incoming calls.

He still manages to read a great deal. He conscientiously looks through the new scores sent to him, though he confesses that it often takes a long time before they are sent back and he still hates deciphering modern scores in unconventional notation. And he prepares his repertory as conscientiously as ever. His technique of preparation, he believes, is perfectly conventional, "I will read the score for a while and then play it at the piano, annotating it with red, green and blue pencil. I make more and more markings, and then at the end of that I know the piece so well I can just as easily take a perfectly clean copy if I have one to perform from. Though I am happy to be working in a country where the conducting from memory lunacy has not reached such staggering proportions as in America, I promise you that by the time I am at the Royal Festival Hall, I could get through the piece from memory. But I see no reason to gamble."

His success as a television performer comes from his natural ability to relax before the cameras, to be his natural, very articulate self. André Previn does not adopt different personae for his different activities, amazing as that may be when you remember their range, from dining at Downing Street to clowning with Morecambe and Wise. It was no mere search for publicity—even if for the LSO's sake he appreciated the sure benefits—that led him in 1971 to invite the Prime Minister, Edward Heath, to conduct the orchestra at its annual gala benefit concert. Mr Heath had been the first chairman of the LSO Trust, and resigned only when forced to by becoming Prime Minister. On social occasions Previn had had plenty of chance to talk seriously about music and about conducting with Heath, and conceived the idea that he might be willing to conduct the orchestra. Before he extended the invitation he asked advice, and it was characteristic of him that before the

Opposite.
Above: Rehearsing in the Great Hall of the Moscow Conservatoire, April 1971. [Mary Lawrence

Below: A Japanese tribute: Previn conducts the LSO at the Osaka Festival, April 1971.

49

performance at London's Festival Hall in November, 1971, he made an extraordinarily elegant speech of introduction; witty and apt and neither patronising nor sycophantic. He was just himself.

That same concert brought the first performance of his own Guitar Concerto, written for John Williams. Previn still makes sure of finding time to compose, not because he believes he is writing great music—he knows he is an interpreter first and a creator second—but because he enjoys it. Hard as the work of composing is, it fulfils a still unsatisfied streak in an ever-questing personality. It is significant that in his *Who's Who* entry (recreations: collecting contemporary art, fencing, American folk art) he lists meticulously his later music from the Symphony for Strings of 1965 onwards, largely ignores the serious music he wrote before. Tackle him direct on his own music, and he will brush it aside, but plainly it matters.

His relationship with William Walton stems in part from a sharing of creative experience. I saw them together on the Russian tour where, with Susana Walton as an ever-sparkling companion, we talked endlessly of music and its practitioners. Previn, like direct contemporaries such as Colin Davis and Bernard Haitink, keeps a very open mind about new music, but finds a barrier after a certain point. He will not perform music he does not feel because it would simply involve getting musicians to play notes accurately and no more. But conversely the music of Walton is something with which he can identify totally. It was a high peak of his career with the LSO when on 28 March, 1971 he conducted at Walton's 70th birthday con-

Below: Congratulating the Prime Minister: the LSO's Gala Concert at the Royal Festival Hall, November 1971.

Opposite.
Above: Music on television— lighter side: Previn with Britain's comedy duo, Morecambe and Wise, in the latter's Christmas Night show, 1971. [BBC

Below: 'American Music and all that Jazz' on BBC television. [Mary Lawrence

HORN
5

cert at the Royal Festival Hall. As a centrepiece the composer himself conducted for Yehudi Menuhin in his Viola Concerto, but the climax of the occasion came when Previn directed a searing performance of the oratorio, *Belshazzar's Feast*. Afterwards, when Walton had received a standing ovation, he went backstage, and Previn asked him to inscribe his score. Tongue-in-cheek as ever even at moments of profound emotion, Walton inscribed it to: 'André, King of Kings'.

The following day, Walton's 70th birthday, found Previn and the LSO and LSO Chorus recording *Belshazzar's Feast* for EMI in Kingsway Hall. The Prime Minister was honouring the composer with a dinner at Downing Street, but Walton insisted on attending the recording session till the very last minute possible. What did it matter keeping a Prime Minister waiting, especially a musical one who understood the priorities?

Previn's establishment as a potent figure on the British musical scene is now assured. His regular performances on BBC Television—always with the LSO, as he insists; his direction of South Bank Summer Music from the season of 1972; his recording contract with the British company EMI which has added warmth to his image on record; his intensive seasons with the LSO not to mention his devotion to British music, Britten and Tippett and many others as well as Walton and Vaughan Williams—all this has given him a base of a greater strength than he has known till now. There is now little danger of his ever again appearing as a chameleon character, particularly when his interpretative powers manifestly intensify and deepen from year to year.

At home in Surrey he searches for relaxation. He plays records—but never for studying interpretation, always for straight enjoyment—and so that he can divide work from leisure even at home, he goes to a separate cottage, ten yards away from the main house, and there at all hours of day and night he works whether at desk or keyboard. "I have to kid myself I'm going off to work like anyone else." The temptation is to stay and play with the twins all day, "the main concern of my life, irresistible, funny and good company", and that is something he can always share with Mia even when the conflicting schedules of their careers keep them separated for weeks· on end. That was a problem they always knew they would have to face, and it makes them enjoy all the more the time they can still share together— as when Mia went with André to the Iceland Festival in the summer of 1972. As he puts it, summing up the contentedness of his existence: "To me waking up in the Surrey countryside with silence, green silence, all round me is a thrill that renews itself every morning."

That expression of contentment brings with it no suspicion of self-satisfaction. There are few musicians of his eminence who are so patently ready to learn from others. A discussion with Previn even on Beethoven's Ninth Symphony will not be a one-way affair, and his deepening responses reflect his ability not merely to convey a composer's purpose as intensely as he can but to look at himself at the same time dispassionately. Players in the LSO may note that at a particular point of his career with them Previn learnt for example how to extract the most delicate pianissimo string tone.

His later records of Vaughan Williams symphonies amply attest to that, and particularly striking are the long drawn diminuendos into nothingness at the ends of movements. It is no criticism whatever to say that this is a quality which emerged: the important point is that he had learnt a lesson and applied it.

As Previn is ready to admit himself, he is still a young conductor in terms of years before the concert-going public. But as his career proves at every turn, his grounding could hardly have been more thorough. His father's insistence on sight-reading, his guidance of his son through the classics, the help of Szigeti and others, the practical experience in the studios of working intimately with an orchestra, both writing and conducting—these and other aspects of his musical education gave him a unique training. An important point to emphasise too is that preparing a film-score, glossy in the end result perhaps, involves very searching musicianship indeed if the man in charge is conscientious, and going to produce a committed result. As Previn says himself: "Standing up before the most faultless musicians two or three times a week, all of them sight-reading, gave me rather a good technique in ferreting out mistakes, working very quickly when time was at a premium, and trying not to bore the orchestra or be self-indulgent. Granted that the music was third-rate, the training was very good. I like to think I work fast with orchestras, and I am sure that that is because I did all that work in commercial media."

"I learn a lot of scores very fast," Previn explains, "though I don't have a photographic memory. There is a certain kind of music with which I am not totally sympathetic—astringently atonal, serial or extravagantly electronic—and it's just a matter of slogging through it. But if it is music that speaks to me, I seem to learn very fast."

Just what music speaks to Previn most vividly is clear enough in essentials from his recorded repertory. He likes colourful music, and that often means, as he says, that "I like music with a strong nationalistic flavour". His success in interpreting Russian music from Tchaikovsky to Shostakovich is witness of that, but equally so his devotion to the brilliant, glittering music of France and of course to the music of the Anglo-Saxon countries. With glowing affection he will bring out the 'local colour' in Copland or Vaughan Williams, but such is his commitment—as his Vaughan Williams records make plain— and his scrupulous concern for detail in the score that the result transcends merely national boundaries, sounds freshly universal.

The question clearly arises, when colourful music provides such a major interest, whether that bespeaks a limit in Previn as an interpreter. After all, you might say that the man who can make second-rate film music sound as intense as the Missa Solemnis is guilty of a confidence trick. In fact the opposite is true. If he can give intensity of performance to ephemeral music, then prima facie his response to the challenge of greater music will be just as intense, for the quality of concentration is what matters. Anyone who has worked with Previn knows that his technique is the opposite of flashy, his approach to music thorough and dedicated, never scrappy. His work is inspirational not out of 'hope-for-the-best' carelessness but as a result of his own magnetism after the most painstaking preparation.

The clue, I feel, to his interpretative approach to music lies not so much in his natural and immediate response to the colourful music with which his name is associated, as in his devotion to Mozart. Asked by a television interviewer what music 'gave him the greatest kick', he did not respond to the question as his questioner plainly intended. Instead he became serious. "Shall I get philosophical for a moment?" he asked. "I couldn't do without the music of Mozart. To me Mozart's music has whatever I'm looking for. If you want it to be dramatic, it is; if you want it to be sensual, it is—roman-tic, virile, angry or calm, whatever you want as a mirror to your emotions."

That response, Previn explained, applied to his feelings not just as a con-ductor and as a listener, but as a pianist too. "I would rather play Mozart than any other composer", he said, and certainly his direction of the Mozart C minor Piano Concerto from the keyboard, which I heard myself many times over on the tour of Russia and Japan, provides the most heady proof of his insight and devotion. His central love of Mozart also helps to explain the stylistic consistency of his performances in whatever field. Where a simi-larly versatile interpreter like Leonard Bernstein—with whom Previn shares many qualities—plays the piano in a strikingly different style from the way he conducts even within a single concerto, Previn to a remarkable degree is consistent. That consistency spreads—perhaps surprisingly—to his jazz piano work. His amazingly sharp definition of finger-work, particu-larly in elaborate ornamentation or passage-work, his 'lifting' of what on paper is merely metrical rhythm, his artistry in giving an individual turn to a phrase, not too little nor too much—these are pianistic qualities that domi-nate both his classical and his jazz playing, and which are naturally translated into his work as a conductor, give his interpretations many of their individual qualities.

If till now his name has been associated most closely with colourful and romantic music, and his emotional warmth as an interpreter cannot be doubted, the root of his approach to the interpretative process as reflected in these performance characteristics digs firmly down to classical sources. Conducting as he does over a hundred concerts a year, mainly with the same orchestra, his repertory is inevitably enormous and grows substantially every year. He is not a man who at one go will take on the symphonies of Bruck-ner, but neither will he fly back in alarm. When he tackles a supreme master-piece like Beethoven's Ninth Symphony for the first time with his own orchestra, he prepares carefully and devotedly, very sure of what he is aiming to do but surprisingly humble in face of the task ahead. The result, as we saw at London's Royal Festival Hall in May 1971, was a spiritual experience of a kind that points very clearly to the future.

The immediacy of Previn's personality, his utter refusal to look down from on high in any human contact, may get in the way of his reputation as an important interpreter of the central classics, the sort of musician who by tradition becomes a musical father-figure. The precise nature of his interpretative image as he develops may present problems—no longer a 'kid-brother' figure, as Steve Previn puts it—but his great asset is that for all his easy-going appearance, there is steel underneath, a thrusting ambition. "If it's successful when I conduct, I must say it makes me terribly happy, and I want to do it again. But when it's unsuccessful, I want to do it even sooner."

As he admits himself: "I probably have a sick amount of ambition." He would find it intolerable if the results of his hard work were not sufficiently good to replenish his ambition, to replenish his apparently inexhaustible supply of energy. But this is ambition working in a character, who very obviously possesses charisma. That charisma he cannot himself explain, any more than others can who possess it. Put it in terms of 'box-office appeal' and he will give a severely practical answer: "For whatever combination of reasons at this time of life I seem to be able to attract people to concerts. I am not so cynical as to think that it's necessarily going to go on for ever. But it pleases me very much if a concert I give of unusual music attracts a full house: that the combination of the LSO and me has a particular appeal. I am delighted that together we have become identified. It can do nothing but good if together we can take music to the mass media."

Steve Previn, himself an expert in box-office appeal, puts it more simply. His brother, he feels, is a musician with whom an audience can identify. Where a magisterial conductor will attract a stiffer audience, André Previn will make music-lovers, whether blue-jean kids or hardened concert-goers, share in the excitement of being a conductor, of making music with a fine orchestra.

The quality is there: the promise holds no limit.

Lunchtime at the local: André with Mia, Matthew (the drinker) and Sascha. Mia had just injured her hand during the run of Barry's 'Mary Rose' at the Shaw Theatre.
[David Hart

✣ The Records ✣

JAZZ PIANIST EXTRAORDINARY

To make a detailed survey of André Previn's early recording career would take a book in itself. By his own calculation his records made during his Hollywood period in various fields—jazz piano, classical piano, film-scores—amount to well over a hundred. When he hears most of them in whatever form—even in a late-night movie on television—he winces and turns in the other direction. When as a reflection of his increasing reputation, some of his earliest jazz records were reissued by Polydor, his main concern was that the date of recording should be made clear, that they should be judged as early work merely.

Many of the tracks stand up remarkably well to re-hearing. Even in 1945 and 1946 when the various items of *Previn at Sunset* were recorded, he had a way of commanding attention in the very first notes with his sharply defined touch, the clarity of definition in flurries of baroque elaboration. A number like *Body and Soul* demonstrates the regular Previn trick of taking a slow song and improvising a very fast piece on it. It is marvellously exciting even if by the end of four minutes the pianist is obviously sweating. The solo piano tracks and those with guitar and bass accompaniment are markedly more imaginative than the two for larger combinations. The piano solo, *Variations on a Theme*, already shows Previn mixing his genres, with hints of Debussy and Hindemith in the unswung opening passage, a highly individual jazz development and a coda back in straight rhythm.

One needs to hear only a few seconds of *My Fair Lady* to register the difference between the earliest Previn jazz discs and the work of Shelly Manne and his Friends in 1956, its extra originality. The performances clearly convey the excitement of the three musicians as in their extended session they discovered each show-number in turn and promptly improvised. Previn's fanfare motif at the very start of the first number, *Get me to the church on time*, is as gentle as could be, but the electricity is at once generated at full voltage, the quality of 1945 projected more subtly. That first track at once grabs the listener by the throat, and through all eight improvisations that is so, whether they are sweet and gentle like *On the street where you live* and (amazingly remembering the stage show) *With a little bit of luck* or riproaringly tense and brilliant like *Wouldn't it be loverly* ('a swinger with echoes of rhythm and blues and the gospel style' says the sleeve) and the *Ascot Gavotte* ('up tempo').

It was not surprising that the enormous success of the *My Fair Lady* disc was followed up with a whole series, but the three friends never surpassed that first excitement, even if at times they equalled it. Maybe the classically oriented listener is bound to register Previn's piano as the primary source of imagination. I must certainly register that response myself, and such a record as *4 to Go* of 1963, in which Previn is joined not only by Shelly Manne but by Herb Ellis and Ray Brown, shows wonderful developments in the fantasy of Previn's jazz invention. As ever the delicacy of fingerwork is one of the trademarks, with a fluttering figure—almost baroque in its elaboration —at the start of the first number *No moon at all* that has a magic akin to Vladimir Ashkenazy's in a very different field. On the same disc *You're impossible* brings characteristic repeated note figures and bunched fistfuls of chords, and an improvisation on one of Previn's own songs *Don't sing along* brings a neat reversal of the usual Previn trick of superimposing triple rhythms across common-time barlines. The basic 12/8 is cunningly disguised for a while by the pianist in his offbeat accents implying square rhythm.

Even more original—at least if heard from a classical base—is one of Previn's own favourites among his jazz records, his collection of improvisations with the trombone player, J. J. Johnson, on songs of Kurt Weill. There very clearly is a comparably intense artist, comparably imaginative, who can inspire and be inspired by his partner as well as by the Weill original. It is fascinating to find in the *Bilbao Song*, for example, from *Happy End* how Previn and Johnson let the harmony get stuck in a groove—one of Weill's own tricks—but use the device for an utterly different end. The actual timbre of the trombone makes for marvellously tough, dark music, particularly when Johnson is cunning as an artist to reserve his tonal strength for the right moments. In the improvisation on the overture from *Dreigro-schenoper* Johnson uses the trombone brilliantly to convey the feeling of a whole range of Weill instrumentation (intuitively he did not for know the original) and in the *Barbara Song* from the same work the sweetness of both instruments belies their usual characteristics. As for the most famous number, *Mack the Knife's Moritat*, the partners daringly adopt a seemingly impossible course in jazz, Johnson working on the theme in the key of C, Previn in the farthest distant key possible, G flat. The result may have something a little contrived about it in its grinding dissonance, but the flair and imagination are inescapable.

When Previn started producing the scores of film musicals, conducting them as well as orchestrating, naturally MGM promoted records from the sound track. They make a long list. One of my personal favourites—and that, I admit, largely because of the work of Cole Porter rather than of the arranger—is of *Silk Stockings*, Porter's musical adaptation of the Ninotchka story, of the implacable but glamorous Soviet woman commissar won over by Parisian decadence. Porter is brilliant at encapsulating the situation ("Is this what is known as the courtship?" asks Ninotchka in a love scene) but has

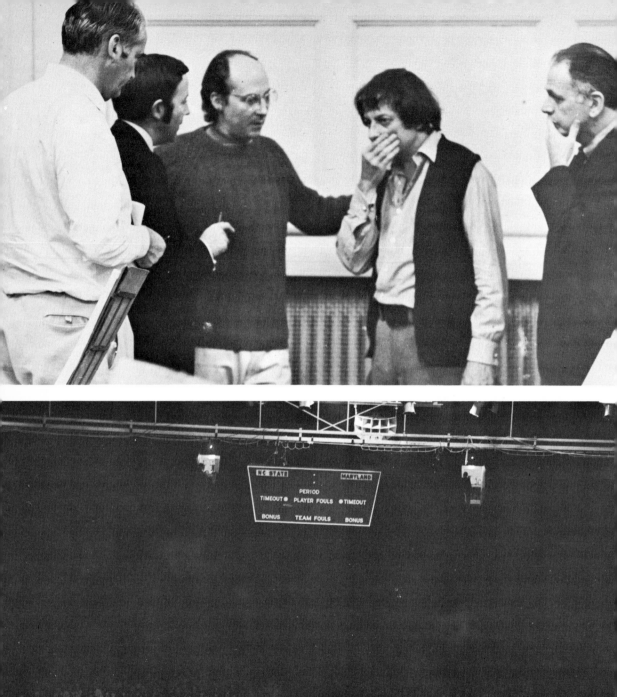

side swipes at phenomena (strictly anachronistic) such as wide-screen cinema and stereophonic sound. Previn nicely points the spiky descant to Fred Astaire's first sweet number *Paris loves lovers* by having it on woodwind and then pizzicato violins even before Cyd Charisse (or rather her vocal stand-in, Carol Richards) uses those phrases for Soviet comment. It is Cyd Charisse, far too sweet, not remotely Garbo-like, who lets down the whole entertainment, and one is grateful for the comparative toughness of Janis Paige in the very funny *Stereophonic Sound* number, a duet in which Astaire is given the couplet "The customers don't like to see the groom embrace the bride, unless her mouth is scarlet and her lips are five feet wide." ('Bosom', incidentally, not 'lips', in the original stage show). A fine brassy setting of that point number by Previn, with a rousing pay-off.

Other major offerings of Previn's peak as a Hollywood composer in the mid-fifties include *Kiss me Kate*, in which the opening ballet number *Too darn hot* gave him welcome scope to make use of his jazz experience. At this time he was using solo instruments to contrast with the generally luscious textures of a Hollywood musical score—solo piano for the start of *So in love*, even a mandolin (no doubt much amplified) in the bright rhythmic number *We open in Venice* with jingling trimmings on percussion.

Previn's career as a Hollywood orchestrator and conductor of film scores had a spectacular epilogue in *Thoroughly Modern Millie*, which he did for Universal well after he had generally given up the film world. He returned, largely out of regard for Julie Andrews and a promise he had made to her several years earlier. Hearing the record is to have the 1922 atmosphere of the film brilliantly re-created, particularly in the title number with its echoes of genuine 'twenties instrumentation (no sousaphones, though, as far as I can judge). Maybe it is not Previn's fault, but as the story progresses so the 'twenties-style trimmings seem to be left behind in favour of latter-day stereophonic opulence. A good score all the same.

Of Previn's original film-scores I have already commented on *It's always fair weather* of 1955, but in 1962 a record was produced—now rather rare—containing the bulk of his score for *The Four Horsemen of the Apocalypse*. It is fascinating to find that the title music, grim and war-like, brings striking similarities with the *Comedy Overture* of 1960 (more recently recorded by the Leicestershire Schools Symphony Orchestra) in the flavour of sharp discords, the flourish of horn motifs, the Shostakovich-like single-note ostinatos and the wide-spaced textures. In the love music Previn shows his fondness for chamber textures inside the big orchestra sound, and in the tender passage entitled *The Key* he has clear Vaughan Williams echoes on solo violin and viola with bare fifths and parallel chords. An echo of Walton with a touch of Hindemith for the movement entitled *Resistance* in a brilliant fugato, clear descendent of Walton's *Spitfire Fugue* and of the *Henry V* music too. A good, striking score, orchestrated with brilliant professional skill.

Even after Previn was well clear of Hollywood and was already installed as principal conductor of the London Symphony Orchestra, he made an important if momentary return to his old world of popular entertainment with the Broadway musical, *Coco*, based on the life-story of Coco Chanel, the fashion designer, and intended as a vehicle for Katherine Hepburn. The record of the show was made three months before the Broadway opening on 18 December, 1969, and was not conducted by the composer. Nor did Previn do the orchestrations which were left in the enormously experienced hands of Hershy Kay, Bernstein's collaborator and helper. The result is a mixture, not surprising when the principal character cannot sing a note. A number like *The money rings out like freedom* has a long-distance echo of Cicely Courtneidge in military mood, and is none the worse for that, when Alan Jay Lerner's lyrics are as skilled as the music. It is disappointing that the intended campness of the tango *Fiasco* for the effete designer, Sebastian, is underplayed, but that is clearly a fault of performance rather than of music or lyric. The square dance routines of *Orbach's Bloomingdale's, Best and Saks* bring a characteristically bouncy ensemble number from Previn. The tunes are attractive but for the most part do not grip the throat. How could they with Hepburn?

Bridging the gap between these records from the pop world and those classically based are two discs in which Previn accompanies opera singers in popular repertory, including a number of his own songs. The first disc, issued by American Columbia in 1962, has Previn—pianist, conductor, arranger and composer—in partnership with Eileen Farrell. The pity is that the voice is so heavily overamplified with help of echo chamber. One of the Previn songs *Just for now* has languid, slow-changing harmonies and attractive autumn imagery in Dory Previn's lyrics ('barren is the bough'). *Where I wonder*, again with lyrics by Dory and music by André, is more sophisticated, with even a hint of Copland open-space music in the use of oboe in the introduction. Here one can compare Farrell's heavyweight reading with the much more delicate handling of the same song on the comparable record that Previn made in 1967 with Leontyne Price—an opera star who had included among her first successes the role of heroine in Gershwin's *Porgy and Bess*.

The range of Price's expression is far wider than Farrell's, lighter and fresher, and the contrast comes out even more clearly in another number common to both discs, *A sleeping bee* with lyrics by Truman Capote and music by Harold Arlen. Where Farrell uses a pushing style, the Wagnerian soprano doing an imitation of Judy Garland (effectively to undermine any chances of the accompanist sparkling much), Price uses a coaxing voice, delectably pointing the words with occasionally smoky tone. For a number like *My melancholy baby* Price uses a sultry tough voice (beautifully set in contrast by the baroque ornamentation of Previn's piano), but her range of tone is wittily brought out, when in another song by the Previns, *It's good to have you near again*, she does what in effect is a Gertrude Lawrence imitation, affecting a Coward plonking accent with English-sounding tone ("You're just a little old, my love, to blame it on your youth").

Previn's first discs in the classical field were as a pianist. One of the earliest, made in 1958 for Contemporary Records, the company which two years earlier had its success with the jazz *My Fair Lady*, is of Chausson's Piano Quartet with members of the Roth Quartet. It is a fine piece with less meandering than one might expect from this composer, but Previn's contribution with rhythms finely pointed and naturally expressive phrasing in the charming slow movement (*Très calme*) is not helped by backward balancing of the piano. The recording producer was Vernon Duke, another composer who bridged the gap as Previn did between the different musical worlds of Los Angeles. The record was one of a series he was sponsoring under the ominous title of Society for Forgotten Music.

French music also played an important part in the solo piano records that Previn made for American Columbia. One of his discs has a coupling of Poulenc and Roussel, with the rhythmic jazz inflections in the writing of both composers superbly pointed as one would expect. The apparently spontaneous flexibility of his piano style brings moments of genuine *frisson*, and tautens perceptibly the 'unabashed sentimentality' of such a piece as Poulenc's *Mélancolie*. For the *Suite Française* he uses a deliberately simpler, less sophisticated style, and the *Presto in B flat* is characteristically marked by light and crisply defined fingerwork. Roussel on the reverse (*Trois Pièces, Sonatine*) is rightly presented in a tougher, brighter light.

Another Columbia disc, made rather earlier, has one of the greatest modern piano sonatas, Hindemith's Third, in a performance full of flair. It misses some of the gentler half-tones in the slow opening movement (very comparable to the first movement of Beethoven's Opus 101) but presents the two fast movements, the typical common-time scherzo and the final elabo-

Calling for order: Previn records Prokofiev's 'Alexander Nevsky' at Kingsway Hall, 1971. [EMI/ Reg Wilson

rate fugue with wonderful incisiveness and drama. Samuel Barber's *Four Excursions* of 1944 similarly seem designed exactly for Previn as pianist, with boogie-woogie overtones in the first (Previn straightening out his normal jazz style by a delicious fraction) and charming variations on *The girl that I marry* in the third.

Another of Previn's solo piano records for Columbia made in the early 1960s has in fact found its way across the Atlantic, a recital entitled—rather misleadingly—*Piano Pieces for Children*. Previn's Mozart here (*Variations on 'Ah! Vous dirai-je Maman'*) has no charm whatever, but gives off electric sparks with the right-hand figuration so crisply defined it reminds one of harpsichord tone. Mendelssohn too (*Six Children's Pieces*, Opus 72) is allowed little charm, but the freshness, even fierceness drives away all hints of sentimentality. After that rather surprisingly Previn conveys a Mendelssohnian lightness in Mussorgsky's *Ein Kinderscherz*, but even there one finds a hint of mechanical stiffness very unlike Previn at his best. On the reverse is a curiosity, a collection of simple piano pieces by Goddard Lieberson, director of American Columbia and a tireless advocate for others' music. Previn sight-read them, unaware that his playing would be put on permanent record. The result has all the freshness one would expect, the simple musical jokes (*How to Handel a Bach Violin Solo*, *Shostakovich's Vacation on a Collective Farm*) presented with the utmost amiability.

Even so such a record does not really represent the best that Previn could achieve at this time in the early sixties. Nor does the Contemporary record of Ernst Toch's Piano Quintet in which Previn is joined by the American Art Quartet. This is gritty, well-made music that one feels one should admire in spite of its generally unlovable exterior. The works of Toch (for a short time Previn's composition teacher) figure prominently in this same Contemporary Composers Series, but this is the only one to which Previn contributed.

Far more representative of Previn's quality as a concert pianist is his record of Shostakovich's Piano Concerto No. 1 which he made with Leonard Bernstein and the New York Philharmonic, though its coupling as a mere fourth-side fill-up to Bernstein's account of Shostakovich's Seventh Symphony *Leningrad*, was unfortunate for Previn. It is a brilliant, spontaneous-sounding performance, with the same sort of rhythmic nudging and crisp-fingered fantasy that one finds much later in his EMI record of Gershwin.

But already Previn had made his first record for CBS as a serious conductor, directing the St Louis Symphony Orchestra in Copland's Suite *The Red Pony* and Britten's *Sinfonia da Requiem*. Granted that the St Louis trumpet soloist in the central scherzo of the Britten is not quite as brilliant as he should be, and the whole orchestra is at this point taxed to the very limit and maybe beyond, the performance hangs together superbly. One is never in any doubt of the conductor's urgent purpose, even if at times in his anxiety he underlines expressive points a little too heavily. That bounding energy carries one similarly through Copland's comparatively long selection of his music for the film-setting of Steinbeck's story *The Red Pony*. The performance reminds one less of Previn than of Bernstein in such music, for the big melodies come near to wearing the heart on the sleeve, with points underlined which very soon after Previn would have allowed to speak for themselves.

Even so the St Louis record makes very plain that here is a conductor who on disc can convey his personal electricity. It is not surprising that when CBS failed to follow up its success—the reasons already explained—RCA took the opportunity of engaging him to conduct for concertos in London. With Lorin Hollander and the Royal Philharmonic Orchestra he recorded the Khachaturyan Piano Concerto, and though the opening has little of the sharp-edged attack one expects of Previn, he quickly recovers and works up a fine energetic performance. The slow movement (no flexatone included) is taken massively, no subtlety allowed to admittedly unsubtle music, and the finale again, despite the urgency, is not quite so crisp of ensemble as one might expect. The fill-up is a rarity, a showpiece for Hollander, the previously unrecorded *Scherzo Fantasque* of Ernest Bloch, a strong confident performance that lacks the last degree of refinement.

For his other concerto record, again with the Royal Philharmonic, Previn had for soloist Leonard Pennario, much more experienced than Hollander in recording. These are performances of Rachmaninov's First and Fourth Concertos that come up surprisingly well when heard today in juxtaposition with the Ashkenazy/Previn versions on the Decca label. If they failed to make their impact initially, it is largely because at key moments (say the very opening of the first concerto) they fail to bring a rush of adrenalin. Previn's Rachmaninov style was already most assured, particularly in the subtle, unexaggerated shading of dynamic. In a way his failure immediately to make his mark in this record reflected his determination to underplay, not to vulgarise music that can easily be sentimentalised. Happily his achievement was not under-appreciated by the promoters of RCA back in New York. They commissioned him to do his first record with the LSO, and from then there was no looking back.

LSO CONDUCTOR

It was André Previn's meeting with the London Symphony Orchestra that marked the turning point of his career as a conductor. From then on it was apparent to public and critics alike that here was a major recording artist, one who deserved judgment on his own terms without reference—good or bad—to his previous career. In particular it marked the beginnings of a love affair between conductor and orchestra, for Previn's first recording sessions with the LSO in August 1965 at Walthamstow Assembly Rooms—favourite haunt of RCA—established the affinity, made him at once a favourite recording conductor with the players. When one remembers how many virtuoso conductors this orchestra works with in recording studios every year, that immediate recognition against all the portents is remarkable.

The first result of the partnership was a version of Shostakovich's most

Rehearsing a concerto at the Bishopsgate Institute: Previn with Arthur Rubinstein. [Mary Lawrence

recorded symphony, the Fifth, which still stands as a model of fidelity to the score—shirking none of the problems while conveying clearly Previn's own concept of the work as "a study in extremes". It was not surprising that he was able to bring out the brilliance of the second and fourth movements. What marked out Previn's quality at once was the intensity of the slow first and third movements. As Jeremy Noble said in an enthusiastic review in *The Gramophone* (May 1966), he did not make things easier for himself in the great measured opening section "by simply taking the music faster as most conductors do". Noble noted a "habit of over-punctuating à la Maazel before important points", but found the impetus of the first great climax almost overwhelming.

Noble's favourable view was endorsed by critics everywhere, and the achievement is the more telling when one comes to compare Previn's interpretation with those of such rivals as Bernstein, Ormandy and the composer's son, Maxim. In clarity and brilliance Previn and the LSO yield nothing to the others in the second and fourth movements, and for the great long-legged second subject of the first movement Previn drew the purest tone from the LSO violins, less 'soupy' than the American, more finely focused than the Russian. But as Previn said, "the essence of the work lies, I think, in the slow movement, the Largo. Shostakovich is always at his best in slow movements, and this is one of his most profound. I think it should be *very* slow, very elegiac, very lyric. After all a distinctly romantic kind of emotion is involved, and I don't think one can do justice to it through under-statement." True to his word, Previn did make this slow movement the emotional focus of the work. With a slower tempo than any of his rivals, an expressive style that phrases naturally without sentimentality and above all with a depth of *Innigkeit* not often achieved in recordings, he established beyond question his status as an interpreter. True, the finale lacks something of the carefree daring which Previn can inject in live performances, but it has fine clarity and precision, and the wonder is that for almost all its length the record conveys the clear illusion of a live performance, no mere studio run-through.

Most of the same qualities emerged in Previn's other recording of August 1965, a version of Tchaikovsky's Second Symphony, *The Little Russian* (another much-recorded work), which was imaginatively coupled with Liadov's rare and charming set of *Eight Russian Folk Songs*. Reviewing the disc myself in *The Gramophone* (September 1966) I at once noted the inner, introspective quality that Previn inspired in the opening slow introduction. Here was the genuine tension of communication presented without mannerism, and though in the first movement *Allegro*, the ensemble is not as perfect as with some rivals, the *Nutcracker* quality of much of the inspiration, the fantasy of it, is implicit in all four movements, with the *Andantino marziale* taken crisply and lightly. Above all Previn's ability to inject a rhythmic spring into the playing, to point Tchaikovsky's syncopated rhythms with a lift that owes something to jazz but never knocks against the barrier of stylishness, is remarkable. Like Giulini on an earlier and equally stylish version, Previn relaxes with nudging rhythms in the delectable second subject of the finale. After that it is disappointing to find that, like Giulini, Previn sanctions cuts—two tiny ones: 16 bars cut immediately after letter P in the score and a couple of pages in the hectic *presto* coda just before letter R.

Cuts in the score (irritating whether sanctioned by the composer or not) also marked the next major recording which Previn did with the LSO, Rachmaninov's Second Symphony, a favourite work of his. Previn suggested to his present record company, EMI, that this was the first major work he wished to re-record quickly, and this he has now done without any cuts whatever. It was the work which in the LSO's tour of Russia and the Far East in the spring of 1971 seemed to sum up so many feelings every time it was played (six times in all, plus a preparatory performance at the Royal Festival Hall in London). By that time Previn had refined his interpretation still further, opening out all but one of the cuts, but already in April 1966, the date of the RCA recording, it was a finely conceived reading which drew together a lyrical work that in less understanding hands can seem to ramble.

RCA's decision to promote Previn in this work was the more remarkable at such a stage, when that company already had in its catalogue an excellent London-made version by Sir Adrian Boult and the London Philharmonic Orchestra. Previn's achievement in the event rewarded the confidence of the record company. Boult's characteristic habit of understatement still allows for unexpected waves of emotion at key points (as at the climax of the slow movement) and the easy skip and jump of the finale is infectiously jaunty. But in the first movement Previn's interpretation allows more light and shade than Boult's. His phrasing is more deliberately expressive than Boult's, but never goes in for self-conscious shoulder-heaving of the kind which mars (for example) Svetlanov's version with the Bolshoi Orchestra on HMV Melodiya. The refinement of the LSO's playing is in keeping with the interpretation. If there is a moment which sums up Previn's quality it is in the unexpected rich melody which comes as the first contrasting episode in the *Scherzo*. I remember when Previn rehearsed this on the 1971 tour the first violin section whistled ironically through their teeth as though to say with a touch of irony: 'Oh how lovely'. In fact, as the very similar recorded interpretation makes plain, Previn's expressiveness is far lighter and more tender than Svetlanov's at this point, more flowing without a hint of sentimentality, yet it still draws out the implied emotion in a way that Boult's very fast rendering of the melody fails to do. As for the great clarinet melody of the slow movement, taken with extreme spaciousness and hushed intensity, Previn was fortunate, in the absence of the LSO's usual principal at the time, Gervase de Peyer, to have an equally fine artist, the late Bernard Walton of the Philharmonia and later London Philharmonic. It was a pity that the recording, generally of the high refined standard that Decca engineers provided in their contract work for RCA, fails to catch the bloom of Walton's instrument, giving it a hint of sourness. As for the finale Previn matches Boult's skipping rhythms with passionate urgency that acts as a challenge to the LSO's finest virtuosity, producing superbly crisp ensembles, and refined hairpin shading of dynamic.

RCA endorsed the success of this Rachmaninov symphony record by sanctioning in the following year, 1967, a Previn version of the Third Symphony, another work already recorded for them by Boult and the LPO. This is the symphony which Rachmaninov in the mid-thirties wrote for the Philadelphia Orchestra, and there is much to be said for opulent Philadelphian sound in the great string melodies. The composer himself recorded the work soon after its composition with that orchestra, and Ormandy later made a uniquely rich-toned version for CBS. But Previn was already clear in his mind about his Rachmaninov style. As the very start makes plain, he sets more store by contrasts of tone and dynamic than Ormandy does. It is not just the difference of recording quality which accounts for the greater refinement of Previn's version. He keeps more in reserve when the great melody of the second subject emerges. He sounds a degree more wayward, less flowing than Ormandy, lighter and dreamier, and when the entry of the percussion tautens the atmosphere it seems more of an intrusion. In the central *Adagio* Previn's manner is easy, even languid but never sentimental, against the warmth and confident extraversion of Ormandy whose solo violin is fatly prominent. In the finale it is arguable that Previn presses the coda too hard, where Ormandy's richness finds its brilliant culmination, but earlier one notes the extra light and shade of the performance from opulent climax to hushed pianissimo. Previn's fill-up is Rachmaninov's early Fantasy for orchestra, *The Rock*, based on a poem by Lermontov, a comparatively slight piece but here beautifully shaded in dynamic and tension. The advocacy

Opposite: Più mosso! A 1971 portrait. [EMI/Clive Barda

66

of such conductors as Previn has undoubtedly helped to establish Rachmani-nov's growing reputation as a composer of the rarest orchestral imagination, a symphonist far greater than was once thought.

Previn has always conveyed his own enthusiasms for particular composers and schools of music with inescapable vividness. It has sometimes brought on him the accusation of limitation, because many of his most notable enthu-siasms are for colourful, romantic music to overshadow his love of the more sober classical repertory, which everyone takes for granted. A record which has tended to be overlooked, but which certainly reflects a highly individual side of Previn's taste, came as a result of a collaboration with the first oboe of the Philadelphia Orchestra, John De Lancie. It was called "Music from France for Oboe and Orchestra" and includes a work specially written for De Lancie, Francaix's elegant *Horloge de Flore* (*The Flower Clock*), a sequence of seven brief movements, each inspired by a particular flower which blooms at a particular time of day or night. Francaix's evocations are often unex-pected: *Deadly Nightshade* (*Belle de Nuit*) for example, warm and inviting in a major key rather than sinister. Predictably the most delightful are the pointed jaunty numbers like the *Malabar jasmine* in rhumba rhythm with the clarinet intertwining with the oboe and the final *Night-flowering Catchfly* (*Sil-ène Noctiflore*) with its flourishing 'oompah' rhythms suggesting (maybe intentionally) night clubs rather than flowers. In all the movements Previn and his soloist underline the rhythmic point, the atmosphere.

The other first recording on the disc—of Ibert's *Symphonie Concertante*—proves less engaging, but only because the music runs on a little too long for its material. Even so Previn does his best to present it persuasively with no hint of half-heartedness. It is made to sound better than it is with a brilliant attack in the finale, which starts with a barefaced crib from the finale of Bartok's *Concerto for Orchestra*. The fill-up is the Debussy arrangement of two of Satie's three *Gymnopédies*. There the atmosphere is exquisite, marred only by the excessive closeness of the oboe soloist.

Another disc of French music issued in 1967 had Previn returning to the keyboard, for with the brilliant Heifetz pupil, Erick Friedman, he recorded two of the greatest Violin Sonatas in the French repertory, César Franck's and Claude Debussy's. Like the orchestral disc of French music it curiously failed initially to attract the attention it deserved. Thanks in great measure to Previn's essentially spontaneous-sounding piano playing the results have the illusion of live performances, with vital interplay between the artists, one responding to the other's phrases. It is striking, too, that as in his jazz records Previn's fingerwork has a rare clarity of definition even in the most rapid passage-work, as in the main theme of the dramatic second movement, normally just a swirl of sound with the notes pedalled over. In both sonatas, even with the lightest pedalling, Previn makes the piano sing, whether in the cello register of his left-hand thumb or in the upper registers. In the Debussy his improvisatory quality (and that of Friedman) is particularly important, with the second and third movements given unusual lightness in almost Mendelssohnian textures.

Early in 1967 back with the LSO Previn turned to Danish music, the Symphony No. 1 of Carl Nielsen, which he coupled with the impressive prelude to Act 2 of Nielsen's great but neglected opera *Saul and David*. This time he came immediately into competition with Ormandy and the Philadelphia Orchestra, whose version of the same symphony appeared simultaneously on the rival CBS label. On the whole in the inevitable comparisons Previn emerged the winner, for his freshness and spontaneity seemed more apt for this fresh product of a young composer's highly individual imagination than Ormandy's weightier manner. Though Ormandy squeezed the symphony on to a single side, he did it at the expense of omitting important repeats, which Previn took care to observe. Evidently by this time he had learnt his lesson over any kind of cutting. Previn also opted for an unusually relaxed tempo in the slow movement—following up a characteristic he had shown already in his records of Shostakovich and Rachmaninov symphonies. For all his fondness of brilliant music, his love of drawing virtuoso playing from his orchestra, he was never one to press on too hard in slow movements, always allowing his sense of line its full breathing-space.

It was in August 1967 that Previn turned to a different area of the repertory —his first opera recording, and his first recording of Mozart: *Der Schauspieldirektor (The Impresario)*, the amusing one-act piece which has long been neglected on record, mainly, one suspects, because of the problems of putting on disc so much spoken dialogue. For this recording an English translation was used. Dory Previn provided not just a new text for the set numbers but a completely new play tailored for the occasion, "a twentieth century transplantation", as the producer, George Marek (also Vice-President of the RCA Record Division in America) put it. For most tastes it proved a little coy in its humour, rather too joky to be repeated very often on disc. The musical contribution too showed Previn at less than full stretch. In the concert hall he has revealed often enough his keen imagination as a Mozartian, but here it was no doubt a mistake for the recording of *The Impresario* to use not his friends of the LSO but the English Chamber Orchestra, a fine Mozartian band who have made superb records of that composer under Benjamin Britten, Daniel Barenboim and others, but who here sound a little stiff in places, lacking sparkle. For once in a Previn record the personality of the conductor seems to be muted. There are places where the challenge inspires some recognisable electricity (as in the jolly woodwind chirping before the reprise of the overture or the opening of the ensemble at the start of side two) but the whole does not add up to the sum of its beautifully wrought parts. The cast was of the highest calibre with Reri Grist as Mme Silberklang, Judith Raskin as Mme Herz, Richard Lewis as Eiler the banker and Sherrill Milnes (then at the start of his international career) as Buff. Leo McKern was aptly ripe-voiced, taking the speaking role of the Impresario himself.

It is sad that the comparative failure of *The Impresario* project seems to have distracted RCA from using Previn in Mozart or other classical repertory. But even in the Russian repertory, the ground on which his reputation was largely based, his next record brought a performance generally below his usual voltage. This was of Rimsky-Korsakov's *Scheherazade*. Here, even more extremely than in other records, Previn showed his fondness for slow tempi, and one of his ways of rationalising it is to explain that he was intending to say in music "Once upon a time . . ." and to let the Arabian Nights atmosphere spread itself luxuriantly. I have no doubt whatever that on another occasion that formula would have worked splendidly, but his comparative failure here goes to show that success in recording owes much to an almost unanalysable ingredient, the impression of spontaneous communication through the barrier of microphone and loudspeaker.

The opening *Largo e maestoso* (*The Sea and Sinbad's Ship*) is extraordinarily meticulous. Where normally Previn's slow tempi concentration and intensity in plenty, this seems above all analytical. The music fails to flow as it should, even while one admires the detail. It is rather like being taken for a country walk with someone explaining every flower. At least one can say that never on record has this work (inspiration of so many Hollywood film scores) sounded less like a film score. The climaxes are sumptuous in sound, but they do not have the full emotional thrust that generally marks Previn's interpretations of Russian music. That is until the brilliant last movement, with its *Festival at Bagdad* and its *Storm at Sea*. Where throughout the performance one constantly admires the quality of the playing—particularly the tripping deftness of the woodwind, the more pointed at slow tempi—it is as though the whole orchestra had suddenly been treated to champagne before the final movement. In a moment the whole performance is alert and energetic, with surging drama the keynote. The fill-ups are beautifully done too, the Tsar Saltan March made to sound curiously like Walton's Globe Theatre music from the film score of *Henry V*.

BRITISH MUSIC

If Previn can on occasion make Rimsky-Korsakov sound like Walton, that is hardly surprising. British music forms so important a section of his recorded repertory—reflecting his longstanding devotion from school-days onwards—that it demands to be treated separately in a survey of his work as a recording conductor.

I have already mentioned his record of Britten's *Sinfonia da Requiem* with the St Louis Symphony, one of the two items on his first major orchestral disc. But it was not long after he established himself as a recording artist working in London that he determined to pursue his purpose of recording British music much further. He was lucky in securing the co-operation of his American recording company—no easy matter when such repertory is still far too little appreciated outside the British Isles—and paradoxically he knew he had to fight British reluctance to allow any but native conductors to have an "authentic" voice in this music. One of his early record sleeves noted that he was "frankly puzzled" by this attitude. Even so he did not let it worry him, and his first record of British music with the LSO could not have demonstrated more clearly his claims to be considered from the start one of its outstanding interpreters.

It was of Walton's First Symphony, a work which the composer insists has nothing to do with the threat of war, but which nonetheless intensely reflects the increasingly insecure of world the 'thirties, the world in which Previn among others was a potential sufferer as he grew up. It is a work in which the nagging nervous tension exactly suits Previn's urgent temperament. *Presto con malizia* is Walton's mark on the nagging Scherzo, with its persistently misplaced accents and jagged silences. That is exactly the spirit which Previn conveys with superb bite and intensity in this recording made in August 1966. As with others among his early records he was faced with the severest competition. This time his record appeared simultaneously with a rival EMI issue in which the New Philharmonia Orchestra was conducted by a veteran Waltonian who had given the first performances of such works as *Belshazzar's Feast* and the opera *Troilus and Cressida*, Sir Malcolm Sargent.

Previn at home, the author's portrait. [*Edward Greenfield*

Few would have predicted the unanimity with which critics acclaimed the Previn version in preference to the Sargent one, which in EMI's advertisements bore the additional imprimatur of the composer's signed approval. As we now know, Walton himself prefers the Previn interpretation to the Sargent, and he is right. Though Sargent scores points with the delicacy of his lyricism in the lovely woodwind themes of the slow movement and in the 'Last Post' trumpet call of the epilogue, it is Previn's performance which consistently bites the more keenly. That is so not only in the malicious Scherzo but in all four movements, for his control of tension, his building of climaxes has a compulsive quality which rivets the listener's attention. As Previn sees it, this is a young man's music, the work of a 32-year-old, a romantic glorying in fine tunes but not a composer who wanted the listener to sit back comfortably.

Though Previn's earliest essays in recording with the LSO were—as I have noted—exceptionally successful, one can see very clearly his process of maturing as a conductor from studying the sequence of Vaughan Williams recordings which he undertook with the LSO between September, 1967 and January, 1972. For that reason I shall look at the cycle of Vaughan Williams symphonies, which forms the core of the sequence, not in order of composition but in order of recording. Even before Previn had recorded the *Sinfonia Antarctica* (No. 7) at Kingsway Hall in the autumn of 1967, RCA had boldly announced that their brilliant star conductor was going on to record all nine Vaughan Williams symphonies. What they did not bargain for at the time was that EMI would promptly modify its plans to share a Vaughan Williams cycle between its two specialist conductors, Sir John Barbirolli and Sir Adrian Boult, and promote a rival cycle conducted entirely by Boult. Once the announcements had been made, there was no drawing back, and music-lovers are the richer for having two complete cycles that underline the genius of Vaughan Williams in different ways.

Previn's recording of the *Sinfonia Antarctica* is not helped by having spoken superscriptions by Sir Ralph Richardson. I well remember the session at Kingsway Hall, London, when Richardson came along at the end of one morning stint, eager as a boy to learn about the tricks of the recording trade but suffering cruelly from a sore throat. Between lines he would deftly pick up a throat spray and project it in his mouth, and at one point he had the engineers foxed when, having been balanced in standing position, he suddenly sat down to recite as the red light went on. It was one of those occasions when (as is regular practice nowadays) the men in the control room badly needed closed-circuit television. Sir Ralph's fears about his voice—he was appearing in a theatrical run at the time—were not unfounded. The finished record has the superscriptions delivered in so furry a voice it makes one want to clear the throat.

The musical contribution is far more impressive, but one notes at once that Previn's way with Vaughan Williams is balder, less coaxing than Boult's. Boult himself is not an 'expressive' conductor in the way Barbirolli was, but here Previn's approach goes a degree or two further towards clear-headed precision, freshness, simplicity. The *Andante maestoso* of the opening representing in its relentlessly rising climax the surge of heroism is taken as slowly as one can ever imagine it. There is a sense of great power in reserve, though some may feel the actual quality of the music is not quite concentrated enough to sustain such treatment and will prefer the more flowing Boult manner. It is ironic perhaps that in this symphony, based as it is on film music from *Scott of the Antarctic*, Previn the film-composer is less atmospheric than Boult. But that is only another way of presenting the regular contrast that Previn is determined to present the argument as coolly and directly as he can without relying on extra-musical evocations. With Previn in the scherzo one feels comparatively little sense of fun in the penguin music of the trio (surprising when his sense of humour is so keen), but he sees the music as angular and sharp, presenting a consistent musical pattern capped by tough climaxes.

He relaxes readily enough in the fourth movement *intermezzo*—the pastoral woodwind solos inspiring a more consciously expressive style—but the final epilogue, like the central slow movement with its bald ice-bound landscape, could not be more brutally direct. Starting with superb biting brass, the finale brings the most impressive playing on the disc with no apology given, and even the women's choirs introduced as another pseudo-instrumental tone-colour rather than to evoke the shuddering chill of the polar icecap. One is given renewed confidence in the validity of the late Vaughan Williams style, its curiously acid flavour, even if one is not encouraged to enjoy the music as much as one is by Boult.

The next two recordings in Previn's Vaughan Williams cycle came in quick succession in the spring of 1968 (recorded, like the whole of the cycle, in Kingsway Hall) and designedly they were meant to go together on a single disc. First in March came the Eighth Symphony, a performance marked by superb dynamic terracing in the first movement, and a Stravinskian precision in the brilliant scherzo for woodwind alone. Perhaps surprisingly when one

Opposite: Working out what Gershwin really meant: EMI No 1 Studio 1971.
[EMI/David Farrell

remembers the resilience of his rhythms in Tchaikovsky and Rachmaninov, Previn pursues even here his very straight approach.

In April came the first major challenge of the cycle in the Sixth Symphony, the great work which from its first performance in April 1948 had captured the imagination of a wide audience with what seemed like a representation of a world in ruins. The composer's own intentions were not quite as simple as that, and whatever the extra-musical glosses we like to put on the final mysterious slow movement, desert-like in *pianissimo* from beginning to end, there is no doubt of its cogent musical logic, developed as it is entirely from the tiniest musical fragment. The three earlier movements too show Vaughan Williams at his most brilliantly inspired. Previn at his April recording sessions had the advantage of having just given a concert performance with the LSO at London's Royal Festival Hall, and the precision of the playing on the record reflects that. Previn's view of the first movement is tenser and darker than Boult's, with no twinkle of humour in the staccatos of the second subject, instead a continuation of the prevailing sinister mood. Then when at the end of the movement Vaughan Williams transforms his earlier idea into a gloriously expansive melody Previn exaggerates the contrast. There is something rhetorical about its expansiveness, where Boult more readily makes the grand tune seem a natural, fresh development of the earlier part of the movement.

In the slow movement with its persistent anapaestic interruptions, jabbed by trumpets and percussion, Previn is again tougher than Boult. He deliberately avoids expressiveness in the *pianissimos*, concentrating on the widest possible dynamic contrasts. He makes it a disturbing, brutal movement. In the Scherzo he is again sharper, more daemonic, faster not only in the main Scherzo but also in the central Trio with its idiosyncratic saxophone solo. The finale—the biggest challenge of all—sees Previn taking a slightly faster tempo than Boult for the marked *Moderato*, perhaps disappointingly when his control of sustained slow *pianissimo* is so remarkable in so many of his records. The result, with deliberate avoidance of consoling expressiveness, is utterly desolate in its hushed intensity, chill music with all colour deliberately drained away. Previn's comparatively fast tempo for that last movement does at least allow the whole symphony—marked to be played without a break—to be squeezed on to a single LP side, not just an advantage of economy.

Next in the cycle, recorded in March 1969, was the Fourth Symphony, the work which in its closeness of spirit (not to mention date of composition) to Walton's First had one thinking would be closest to Previn's heart. The pity is that the recording does not reflect the quality of interpretation that Previn has since achieved with the LSO in many performances in America and Russia as well as in England. Though broadly the interpretation is consistent with the rest of the cycle, he does not quite convey on record the biting urgency which marks his live performance and which in this of all the Vaughan Williams symphonies one would have expected. There are numerous rival versions here, not least the composer's own first recording transferred by World Record Club from 78s, and one of the disappointments of the first movement is that Previn's tempo, slower than those of the others, makes for less urgency. His refusal to allow 'give' in the rhythm helps to compensate, but to hear Vaughan Williams himself afterwards for all his wildness is to experience something much more violent. So too in the slow movement which with Previn has an icy chill, but which fails to build up to quite the relentless climaxes one expects. The scherzo with Previn is light and precise, even delicate, and after a wonderfully mysterious bridge passage the finale begins a little cautiously. But then it expands in confidence, even though it never quite achieves the fullest dramatic intensity.

The fill-up to the Fourth Symphony disc is unexpected but very welcome, the so-called *Concerto Accademico for Violin and Strings*, a work inspired like so much imaginative violin music of the 'twenties—Ravel's *Tzigane* and the Bartok Sonatas for example—by Jelly d'Aranyi. It remains one of Vaughan Williams' most elusive works, for in effect he was adopting his own personal brand of neo-classicism that for all the occasional pastoral overtones in modal writing is fundamentally as gritty as Stravinsky's. The soloist here is James Oliver Buswell IV, one of the extraordinarily talented group that emerged in the sixties from the classes of the great Ivan Galamian in New York— Itzhak Perlman, Pinchas Zukerman and Kyung-Wha Chung being among the others. Buswell does very well indeed to get inside a difficult, highly personal idiom, and his youthful passion in the slow movement contrasted with stillness and poise is most impressive.

Disappointment with Previn's rendering of the Fourth Symphony is merely comparative. The next in the cycle, recorded within the year in February 1970, was the first and most expansive Vaughan Williams symphony of all, *A Sea Symphony*, in which the LSO was joined by the LSO

Listening to a playback of Vaughan Williams's 'Sea Symphony' at Kingsway Hall, February 1970. L to R Heather Harper, André Previn and John Shirley-Quirk. [RCA Records

Chorus. RCA's decision to squeeze the whole work—well over an hour long—on to a single LP meant that the recording level was lower than usual, but the actual quality of sound is excellent on the right machine, and the performance reinforces the contrasts already noted between the Boult interpretations and Previn's. At the start where Boult's invocation is warm and expansive, Previn's is full of dramatic, nervous energy, and in case that suggests he rushes through the work at high speed with his mind on the engineers' needs, that is not so. Indeed the *Largo sostenuto* of the second movement, "On the beach at night, alone", is markedly slower than in either of Boult's performances on record, HMV or Decca. Previn concentrates on clarity and stillness, and he is helped by a more satisfying soloist in John Shirley-Quirk than HMV provided for Boult. Lightness and clarity again in Previn's Scherzo and wide dynamic contrasts in the Finale are remarkably well conveyed considering the length of side. Heather Harper, Previn's soprano soloist in the *Pastoral* as well as the *Sinfonia Antarctica*, sings here with characteristically creamy tone, and the chorus is in fine incisive form. Altogether, as I said of the London Festival Hall performance which preceded the recording: "One has a feeling of the youthful Vaughan Williams expanding in energy, not in self-indulgence."

With the next in the cycle, No. 9, Previn coupled a work previously unrecorded, the *Three Portraits* from *The England of Elizabeth*. It comes first on the disc, and was in fact recorded as early as March, 1968, almost three years before the symphony. It is unpretentious colourful music with occasional touches of archaic instrumentation and quotations from sixteenth century melodies to add a Tudor flavour. The suite was adapted by Muir Mathieson from Vaughan Williams's film score for a production of British Transport Films in 1955.

It was in April 1958, only a few months before the composer's death at the age of 86, that the Ninth Symphony was first performed at a Royal Philharmonic Society concert under the direction of Sir Malcolm Sargent. Almost universally the critical opinion was that the composer was simply rambling over well-tilled pastures. It took some years before that false view was rectified, first in the performances—live and recorded—of Sir Adrian Boult, and then quite irresistibly in the record made by André Previn and the LSO in January 1971. Even more strikingly than Boult, Previn plays the symphony without apology, seeking not to link it with Vaughan Williams's earlier symphonies but underlining the strange, often gauche contrasts and juxtapositions. At a first hearing they can seem merely signs of rough workmanship, but with Previn very clearly the brutality of the construction is deliberate. After all, perhaps more than the composer knew, this symphony was in some ways anticipating more recent trends in its angular construction.

In the first movement the contrasting of the two main themes is baldly done in alternation, but the result is tough not naive, resolving satisfyingly at the very end. The saxophone choir (nicely balanced by Previn) adds a flavour to the orchestral cooking that had come to delight the old man's ear, and the flugelhorn (with very specific directions given in the score on the correct mouthpiece to use) makes its eerie appearance. The second movement, with its edgily rhythmic passages the antithesis of the conventional easy-going Vaughan Williams slow movement, starts with a flugelhorn solo. It is unconventional, even perverse music but the inspiration of a genius still alert. At the end Previn finds a spiritual quality that reveals something of his own development. The skipping Scherzo is a characteristic product of Vaughan Williams in his last period, with clarinets and bassoons added to the saxophone choir for the trio, and the Finale, though it starts as if it is going to be a 6/8 version of the soft Finale of the Sixth Symphony, develops chunkily until the bald juxtapositions at the end inspire Previn to his finest qualities as a Vaughan Williams interpreter.

The challenge of proving that such a symphony as the Ninth was far finer than had been thought was formidable, but it was the sort of challenge that, as we knew, Previn would accept with relish. The challenge which remained was even greater, and it was one about which even Previn's keenest admirers would not predict too closely. The three symphonies which remained to be recorded were those most personal to the composer, the *London* Symphony (No. 2) which to the end of his life as Michael Kennedy has reported seems to have remained the composer's own favourite; the *Pastoral* (No. 3) and No. 5, which one might unofficially subtitle *The Pilgrim*.

The recording of the *Pastoral*, made in January 1971, at once showed the new spiritual depth of Previn's readings of Vaughan Williams. As I wrote myself in *The Gramophone* of September 1972 (this was the last of the set to be issued just before the composer's centenary), this performance brought home as never before how daring this work is as a symphonic concept with the process of lyrical fusion and regeneration expanded in four measured movements, only one of them, the shortest, even moderately fast. In 1922 when it first appeared (Vaughan Williams had been thinking about it for six years by then), it was no doubt accepted by most admirers as a congenially rambling example of the composer's pastoral manner. It is far more than that, as Previn makes very clear indeed. Boult in his outstanding HMV performance takes care to mould the music at flowing tempi, understandably anxious that such low-contoured plains should not seem dull. Previn's approach is more daring. Accepting the view that this is a great symphony quite independent of evocative overtones, he adopts even slower tempi and refuses to mould them overmuch, relying on simple concentration from himself and his players. This was an approach which as early as the 1965 recording of the Shostakovich Fifth Symphony he had essayed with great success, but the achievement is the more remarkable in the *Pastoral* with playing from the LSO strings as refined as one could imagine, and the subtlest, most precise shading of dynamics over the full range. In Previn's hands this becomes a symphony which in spareness and economy can be compared with such a masterpiece as Sibelius's Fourth.

The coupling provided a complete contrast, and delightfully it introduced in a solo role on record one of the most striking characters of the LSO, the principal tuba, John Fletcher. This was Vaughan Williams's late Tuba Concerto, a pawky work that goes beyond the merely humorous qualities of an understandably neglected instrument. The same performers had great success with this music in a performance on BBC television at the time the record was issued, and here similarly on record Previn, Fletcher and the LSO are able to link the music, whether the gallumphing outer movements or the easy-flowing Romanza, very clearly with the late symphonies.

The Fifth Symphony came next in the recording schedule after the orchestra had returned from its tour of Russia and the Far East in 1971. Though Previn was confident that his recording of the *Pastoral* was his finest achievement in the Vaughan Williams cycle so far, the Fifth provided at least an equal challenge, for though its contours are more clearly defined, it presents equally the inner essence of Vaughan Williams in his reflective modal manner. At the same time it is far better known, and invites immediate interpretative comparisons in most listeners' minds. Again as in the *Pastoral* Symphony Previn takes a cool, measured view of the landscape. The phrasing is more purely shaped, coaxed less than with Boult let alone Barbirolli, and the tempi in first, third and fourth movements are slower. It is the spiritual quality of the music rather than its atmospheric associations—whether with Bunyan, whether with the English countryside—which is underlined. But Previn has seen the essential point of the work to combine the spiritual calm with control of tension over the longest span, above all with emotional fulfilment at the great climactic moments. In the first movement with its spine-tingling modulations and crunching suspensions he matches the emotional intensity that both Boult and Barbirolli convey at these key moments. In the slow movement he goes further. At his slow tempo he builds a structure with compelling intensity that resolves in moments of climax as richly emotional and fulfilling as Elgar's moments of resolution. Nor does he do that with vulgar effect-making and distortion of what is written, merely by following the markings in the score simply and faithfully, adding of course the emotional ingredient that is the magic of the great interpreter.

For fill-up Previn chose *The Wasps* Overture, taken at a characteristically measured tempo, but still full of point and clarity with the great melody of the second subject richly expansive without sentimentality. The beauty of scoring in this overture reflects something of what Vaughan Williams learnt from his studies with Ravel in Paris (strange confrontation of composers in their thirties, the Englishman three years older than his 'teacher').

That orchestral sleight of hand, that ability to write with the finest concern for orchestral balance, which for the rest of his life Vaughan Williams, tongue-in-cheek no doubt, was going to deny in himself, comes out even more magically in the *London* Symphony. Sheer beauty of sound is what first strikes one in Previn's interpretation recorded as the last of the cycle in January 1972. But even as one registers this (partly the work of the recording engineers who have essayed the widest dynamic range with amazing fidelity) one begins to appreciate that Previn is intent on treating the work not as a sequence of programme pictures in music—jingling hansom-cabs, lavender-

Opposite: With John Fletcher, the LSO's tuba-player, before a take of Vaughan Williams's Tuba Concerto, Kingsway Hall 1972. [RCA Records

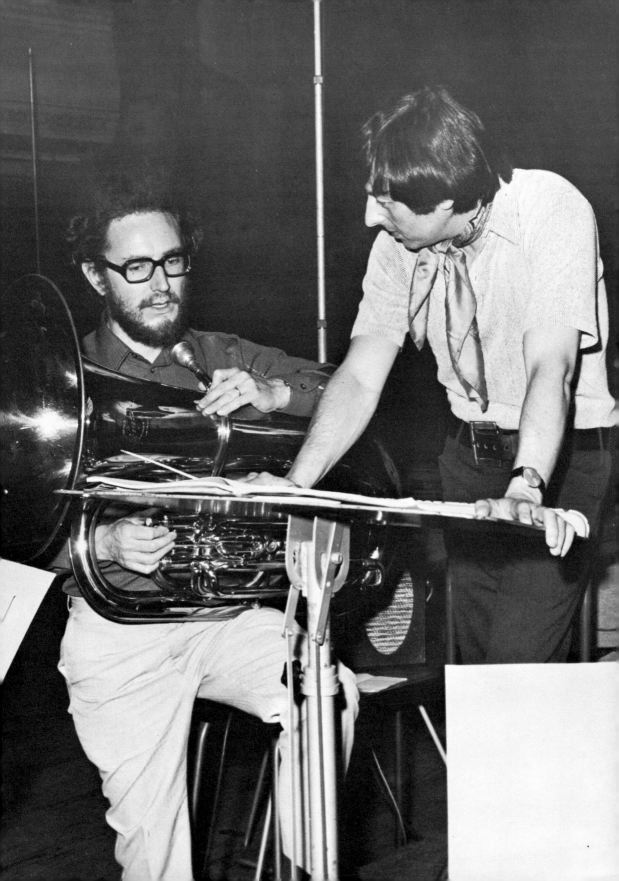

sellers and the like—but as a finely wrought symphony. It is strange to find that in the cake-walk rhythms of the first movement Boult brings more of a music-hall swing to the music, where the syncopations of the ex-jazzman Previn are electrically precise, present much less relation to the popular music background by which Vaughan Williams was undoubtedly inspired. Boult to that extent is more obviously idiomatic—as indeed he is in some of the other symphonies too—but the *London* has never seemed greater as a symphony than with Previn. Over and over again the hush of a pianissimo has one catching the breath, the identity of conductor and orchestra perfectly matched, the ensemble exquisitely controlled with no feeling of constraint but instead a continual sense of concentration, natural and spontaneous, the illusion of live, not canned, music-making.

When RCA first sanctioned the recording by Previn of a complete Vaughan Williams cycle, one of the purposes was to bring this great music more into the main stream of orchestral literature, out of the byways of Englishry. That purpose Previn certainly fulfilled, above all in the three culminating recordings of Nos. 2, 3 and 5. He made one think not of himself but of the greatness of the music.

By the time he had completed the cycle, he had long been established as a British resident, firmly accepted as an essential figure in the energetic musical community of resurgent London. Even his own music had come to feel as though it was British, at least in part. As an epilogue to this chapter on British music, may I mention his recording with the Leicestershire Schools Symphony Orchestra of his own *Overture to a Comedy* of 1960. Although it was written in Los Angeles ("I had great fun putting it together in a very short time", as Previn puts it) and there is an outrageous crib from Bernstein's *Candide* Overture, a favourite work with Previn, it inhabits very much the same world as the comedy overtures of Walton. "I still like approximately two dozen measures of it", said Previn caustically after the recording, but nonetheless expressed enormous admiration for the youngsters' playing of the piece. He promised to write something specially for them, but with his heavy schedule of work pressing continually on him he has still not fulfilled that promise. That piece, when it emerges, one can firmly predict, will be clearly recognisable as British music, the creative work of a unique advocate.

THE WAY TO 'BELSHAZZAR'S FEAST'

It took Previn just under four and a half years to complete his Vaughan Williams cycle for RCA, some achievement when one remembers his concert commitments over that period. The project occupied his main attention during his RCA contract, but the company did manage to record concurrently a number of issues of other music, attractive rather than world-shaking. I have already mentioned Rimsky-Korsakov's *Scheherazade*. A year later in March 1969 he did an unexpected collection of Richard Strauss orchestral music, including the much-maligned orchestral suite which the composer arranged in 1945 from *Der Rosenkavalier* and the first ever recording of an occasional piece of 1939, originally a film-score, the commemorative waltz *München* (Munich).

München has plentiful echoes of *Rosenkavalier*-style waltzes, including one idea that is an almost exact copy of Mariandel's *Schöne Musi'* (lovely music) of Act 3. Even Previn cannot quite disguise the fact that at nine minutes it is rather long for its material. His account of the *Rosenkavalier* suite is interesting in its avoidance of operatic gesture. Previn himself has long explained that though he enjoys opera, he much prefers the orchestral repertory, and here he tackles the sequence of sumptuous moments—including the prelude to Act 1, the Silver Rose scene, the great Act 3 trio and duet and waltzes galore—with little reference to stage tradition. The usual criticism of this suite is that it vulgarises the great opera from which it is derived, but without singers to worry about Previn goes in the opposite direction, and simply lets the music speak for itself. At the opening he may seem a little too careful, but the tenderness, the gentleness of the Silver Rose music is charming, fresh without sentimentality, while the lovely melody which opens the Trio is delicately pianissimo on the oboe with no hint of the *Grande dame* Marschallin. Whatever one thinks of Strauss's arrangement, this is a performance which avoids excessive sweetness so far as is possible. Previn's own favourite item on the disc is *Don Juan*, performed with predictable brilliance and fine swagger, clarity and fearless underlining of dynamic contrast. It is hardly Previn's fault that the violin-tone is not so sweetly caught by the engineers as usual. Curiously enough, one climactic moment is far more operatic in its feel than anything in the *Rosenkavalier* Suite, the great rich entry of the horns towards the end (letter Y) which brings a surprising echo of the Marschallin's entry in Act 3 of the opera.

The other incidental record of the period, made in February 1970, is of Mendelssohn's *Italian* Symphony, coupled very suitably with the Overture *Ruy Blas*, for long an underrated work, and less predictably with Prokofiev's *Classical* Symphony. Again the violin tone is not as sweet as one expects from this source, but all three performances are effervescent. In the first movement of the *Italian* Symphony Previn's fast tempo still allows plenty of light and shade, shaping of phrase and the crispest pointing of staccato rhythms. The exposition repeat is taken to allow the important linking passage to be heard. A good flowing tempo for the Pilgrim's March, giving the illusion of plenty of breathing space; a flowing account to the third movement with the horns of elfland charmingly evoked in the Trio, and fantastic precision in the headlong staccato passages of the final Saltarello. Tenderness at the end too, but without any sentimental rallentando.

Such a performance of a repertory work reflects the brilliant standards which Previn was achieving in his concerts at the time with the LSO, and the same is true of the other two performances on the disc with lightness and clarity marking the Prokofiev symphony as well as the Mendelssohn overture. The unexpected coupling was chosen, it seems, when the Prokofiev was one of the items included in the LSO's American tour immediately after the record was completed.

In live performance at the Royal Festival Hall Previn was his own soloist in more Mendelssohn, the G minor Piano Concerto (No. 1), but for record he contented himself with the accompanying role. His soloist was the young Israeli pianist, Joseph Kalichstein, and as in his own solo performance Previn took an uncompromising view of the work, refusing to present it as a miniature concerto, a small-scale piece. The very opening is tough, and the slow tempo for the central *Andante* gives extra stature to an idea which can sound like a Victorian hymn-tune. As for the finale, some may be disappointed that its whizzing *Molto allegro* allows for comparatively little charm, but its lightness and brilliance are still characteristic of conductor and soloist.

Earlier Previn had also conducted for another talented Israeli artist, the violinist, Itzhak Perlman, who coupled two French concertante works, Lalo's *Symphonie Espagnole* and Ravel's *Tzigane*. Both performances refuse to indulge in atmospheric warmth. In a sense one can compare this characteristic with Previn's underplaying of atmosphere in the Vaughan Williams symphonies, but with such colourful music as this, French composers deliberately creating exotic flavours, Spanish and Hungarian respectively, it is arguable that the music does not relax enough. Even so it is refreshing to have music that is so often treated sentimentally presented with diamond-bright precision of texture in the orchestral accompaniment and sharply dramatic rhythms.

Then with one of RCA's most cherished artists, the guitarist, Julian Bream, he conducted for Villa Lobos's colourful Guitar Concerto. The lightness of the accompanist, the balance, the delicately placed precision, reflects the sympathy of a conductor who was just completing the composition of a Guitar Concerto of his own.

Previn, as an experienced concert pianist himself, finds enormous enjoyment in accompanying others in concertos. That is why, in the contract he signed with the British company of EMI at the end of 1970, he insisted that he would still be free to conduct in concertos for rival labels. He had made much the same arrangement with RCA. For Decca he had already collaborated in an outstanding concerto record with an artist who was very quickly going to establish a special relationship not only with the LSO but with the British public as a whole, indeed the world public—the Korean violinist, Kyung-Wha Chung.

Just as her fellow Galamian pupil and joint winner of the Leventritt award, Pinchas Zukerman, had earlier come to London at short notice to record the Tchaikovsky Violin Concerto (for CBS) so did Miss Chung. In the finished record—she was still only 21 at the time—there may be a hint in her playing in the first movement of tension too pent-up, but that is hardly surprising and it is momentary. What is remarkable about this performance—and equally of the performance of the Sibelius Violin Concerto on the reverse—is the commanding directness of the solo work, which matches the urgently dramatic playing of the LSO under Previn. Like Previn, Miss Chung has the ability to convey without exaggeration of expression the natural intensity of her interpretations. The slow movement of the Tchaikovsky, for example,

Opposite.
Above: Kyung-Wha Chung at her first recording session demonstrates a point after hearing the playback, Kingsway Hall, 1970. [Decca Record Co.

Below: Kyung-Wha Chung introduces Previn to Korean friends after the LSO's concert in Seoul, May 1971. [Mary Lawrence.

may sound cool after some other readings, but the tender simplicity of expression is more deeply moving than almost any. There is similar emotional power in the great lyrical passages of the Sibelius, a work in which Previn brings out the orchestral beauties with the finest precision, judging the power of the tuttis meticulously. As for the finale, Chung and Previn together produce not merely fireworks of a conventional kind but sparks of wit to lighten the general darkness of colouring. It is a magic record, instantly compelling.

The other concerto project which Previn undertook for Decca spanned a broad compass, for with Vladimir Ashkenazy, another artist who has become a personal friend, he completed a cycle of all Rachmaninov's works for piano and orchestra. His previous Rachmaninov recordings for RCA included not only the Second and Third Symphonies but also the First and Fourth Piano Concertos with Leonard Pennario as soloist—one of his first two British-made records. If Previn's conducting was already warm and sympathetic for Pennario, it had grown subtler by the time he was working with Ashkenazy. The differences are partly a reflection of the contrasted styles of the two pianists. With Pennario Previn had a more straightforward task. With Ashkenazy, a poetic interpreter of Rachmaninov even to the point of waywardness, the sheer problem of matching the soloist's rubato, his expressive style, was difficult in itself. Fortunately Previn's own preferences in interpreting this composer point in a very similar direction. It is the delicacy of the playing of the LSO above all which strikes one as remarkable, an unexpected quality in works which are regularly treated as warhorse virtuoso concertos. The many passages marked *espressivo* draw from Previn and his players the most delicate shading of phrase, more complex in its shaping than in the 1964 Pennario performance (which incidentally was with the Royal Philharmonic) but less self-conscious. There is no hint of the emotion being played up artificially. Even the Second Concerto, a work so frequently played it is in danger of becoming hackneyed, Previn and Ashkenazy can make the result sound utterly new. I think for example of the reprise of the main theme in the slow movement just before Figure 26 in the score, a moment of the purest poetry.

In some ways the most remarkable performance of all is of the *Rhapsody on a Theme of Paganini*, which has a liveness, an electricity which reflects the circumstances of the recording. At the Kingsway Hall sessions there was a rehearsal and then simply two straight performances. The sense of spontaneity in the result amply confirms that. Even if ideally one would have liked a more delicate pointing of the final cadence, a touch of wit instead of a plonk (more the task of the pianist rather than of the conductor), that is the only moment which calls for any reservation. The varying moods of the twenty-four variations are held together with wonderful continuity, and the great 18th variation with its broad-spanning melody has the ripest sense of fulfilment, even though soloist and conductor deliberately avoid a vulgar wash of emotion. It says much for these performances that they do indeed work as a cycle. A playing in sequence of all five works brings out their cohesiveness while acquitting the composer of indulging in mere repetition.

It was not until the summer of 1971 that EMI was able to translate its new contract with Previn into completed recordings. Ironically enough the EMI recording manager assigned to the newly enlisted conductor was Christopher Bishop, who over the previous five years working with Sir Adrian Boult on HMV's rival set of Vaughan Williams symphonies had come to look on Previn as 'the enemy', while still admiring his work. From the start it proved an excellent collaboration. Previn and Bishop share an individual brand of black humour, and the test of the relationship could hardly have been more severe than in the first of Previn's recording projects for EMI, the Sitar Concerto of Ravi Shankar. This was the work which Previn and the LSO presented with the composer as soloist in London's Festival Hall in January 1971. The recording followed several months later, but the score with its odd superimposition of the structure of the Indian Raga on Western techniques was still in a fluid state. The experience is rather like hearing a Western orchestra through Indian ears, and though the musical content by Western standards is slight for a piece lasting roughly 40 minutes (particularly when the idiom is pervadingly sweet) the work of Previn and the LSO could hardly be more delicately adroit. There are moments when bathos seems not too far away—as at the very opening when one almost expects the oompah-pah of a waltz after a passage very similar to Weber's *Invitation to the Waltz*. The third movement, the shortest of the four with some attractive, gently Bartokian ideas, is on the whole the most successful, though the fourth movement brings the most imaginative and memorable single moment, a striking interchange between horn, flute and sitar. When one remembers that the composer is not versed in Western notation, the achievement of conductor, orchestra and recording team in presenting so polished a performance to match the composer's semi-improvised solos is remarkable.

The second of Previn's discs for EMI also featured concertante music, but this time he was in the centre of his own field, and for the first time with the LSO on record he was his own piano soloist. The works were Gershwin's *Rhapsody in Blue* and Piano Concerto in F coupled sensibly and attractively with the vivid Gershwin Overture, *An American in Paris*. Though the choice of this repertory for Previn's new contract might initially seem to be belittling his achievement, it was understandable that EMI wanted to begin with a big commercial success. Previn by 1971 had established clearly in the public mind that he was a serious conductor who could range confidently from Françaix to Beethoven's Ninth, but launching him in music the whole world knew was his early speciality, was safer. Every moment of the Gershwin record reflects Previn's own exuberant enjoyment, and that in spite of the inevitable extra problems the conductor has if he is also the soloist. Proving that it was no fluke, and that he really could do both jobs at once,

Directing from the keyboard: Previn records Gershwin with the LSO at EMI's studio in St John's Wood, 1971. [EMI/David Farrell

Previn later featured the Concerto in a brilliantly successful performance for BBC television.

In his solo work both in the Concerto and *Rhapsody in Blue* Previn gives a clear feeling of improvising the music, so flexible is the style of phrasing, so mercurial the execution in the many flourishing virtuoso passages. His utterly authentic style is deliciously reflected in the work of the LSO soloists, with Gervase de Peyer providing nudgingly idiomatic rubato in his opening clarinet solo in *Rhapsody in Blue*, and Howard Snell, the LSO chairman and a brilliant trumpet player, using exactly the right sultry style in the haunting solo for muted trumpet in the slow movement of the Concerto. By one of the tricks common in the record industry, a rival version of the Concerto and Rhapsody appeared simultaneously with Previn's EMI disc (Werner Haas and the Monte Carlo Opera Orchestra under Edo de Waart on Philips) but for all the crispness of execution the contrast of so 'square' a performance served only to highlight the brilliance and imagination of Previn's.

The EMI recording team had an even more taxing problem when it came to Previn's recording of a work for chorus and orchestra, a work which incidentally combined Previn's devotion to Russian music and to film music, the cantata which Prokofiev took from his music for the film *Alexander Nevsky*. As in his performance of Strauss's *Rosenkavalier* Suite Previn seems intent on not conjuring up memories of the original dramatic purpose, but of treating this as a great score in its own right. There is no lack of searing drama in the long sequence of the *Battle on the Ice*, for the relentless ostinato rhythms build up into an overwhelming climax superbly caught by the engineers, and though the LSO Chorus, for all Arthur Oldham's thorough and intensive training, cannot quite give the illusion of earthy Slavonic tone, the incisive attack more than makes up for that. As for the mezzo soprano soloist in the loveliest passage of the work, the lament *The Field of the Dead*, Anna Reynolds makes a welcome contrast in the firm richness of her singing to the unsteady slavonic singers in 'authentic' performances. Some of Previn's tempi for the choruses are on the slow side—so, incidentally, were many of Fritz Reiner's in his Chicago recording for RCA—but in every instance they underline the weight of the music, showing that in musical terms this has risen beyond the limits of an illustrative accompaniment to a film sequence.

It was CBS not EMI or RCA that gave Previn in 1972 his first chance to record an example of his own music with the LSO, the Guitar Concerto which he wrote for John Williams. This was the work which was given its world premiere at the LSO Gala Concert of November 1971 at London's Royal Festival Hall, when Prime Minister Edward Heath's conducting of Elgar's *Cockaigne* took priority in the public eye. The Previn Concerto is an immensely likeable work, full of good ideas and on record given an even sharper, more purposeful performance than it received at its concert-hall première. It starts with a haunting theme from the soloist, sidling in with downward arpeggio phrases, a carefree country-walk melody that sounds even more ravishing when almost immediately it is taken up by the violins of the orchestra. The scoring is light, and the whole movement, just under six minutes, seems to promise a completely lighthearted work in the vein of most Guitar Concertos.

But then Previn changes direction, for the central *Adagio* is altogether weightier in tone, starting as it does with bare string writing that echoes the open-spaces music of Copland and Harris. If it fails to make so immediate an impression it is that the thoughtful tone of voice comes rather unexpectedly. The writing as ever is inventive from first to last, and soloist and composer dedicatedly helped by the orchestra hold together the longish structure —just over ten minutes—with fine concentration. The finale brings an obvious gimmick, but one which on gramophone repetition justifies itself. The soloist starts a musing recitative only to be interrupted by a jazz combo—electric guitar, electric bass guitar and drummer—and at intervals through the movement the conventional forces are thrust away from their reflective *Andante* by these buzzings in the ear. The conventional forces unemphatically work the movement towards a complete enunciation of the lovely Copland-like melody that no doubt was the seed of inspiration for the whole movement. The jazz forces make one final incursion, and quietly the conventional forces return unperturbed, as though to say: "That's enough, boys!" A victory for serenity and order, a passage at the end very reminiscent of some of the haunting musical collages of Charles Ives.

The coupling for the Previn work—a welcome addition to the repertory, far more substantial than most Guitar Concertos—is another longish work, the *Concierto del Sur* (Concerto of the South), by the Mexican composer, Manuel Ponce, a much more conventional piece but delightful with its easy Spanish-sounding tunes. In the *Allegretto* first movement—which takes up exactly half the work in time-length—Previn's accompaniment matches the natural definition of the guitar in its point and clarity, and so it does again in the bright, jaunty finale, while the central *Andante* brings yearningly beautiful string playing, an example of the LSO turning its hand to unpretentious music and still showing its most refined qualities.

The LSO's ability to relax in lighter music with Previn in charge was never more brilliantly demonstrated than in the fill-up they provided together for the live recording made of Edward Heath's Festival Hall account of *Cockaigne*. Heath's remarkable feat—the more impressive when repeated 'cold' on the gramophone—demanded a record, but it was hard to know what would match it. In the end a delightful hotch-potch was worked out, three orchestral showpieces. The first is Leonard Bernstein's Overture *Candide*, played as an encore at the Gala Concert but sounding even more scintillating on record, even more precise, even more exuberant than the composer's own recording. The second is another encore piece, completely contrasted but equally successful in demonstrating the quality of the LSO's work under Previn, Vaughan Williams's *Fantasia on Greensleeves*, delicate and refined in string tone with wonderful playing from the LSO's first flute, Peter Lloyd. Finally a piece which scored enormous popular success for Previn and the orchestra on television and which unaccountably had been

Opposite.
Above: Kingsway Hall: André Previn with the LSO and LSO Chorus recording 'Alexander Nevsky' with Previn. [EMI/Reg Wilson

Below: Arthur Oldham, Chorusmaster of the LSO Chorus, discusses a detail in 'Alexander Nevsky' with Previn and EMI Recording Manager, Christopher Bishop. [EMI/Reg Wilson

Above: Previn and the Yale
Quartet recording at All Saints,
Tooting, August 1972. [Edward
Greenfield

Opposite: Celebrating Sir
William Walton's 70th Birthday
29 March 1972: the composer
looks in on the Kingsway Hall
sessions for 'Belshazzar's Feast'.
[EMI/G. Macdominic

neglected by the record companies, Georges Enesco's *Roumanian Rhapsody*
No. 1—a delectably swaggering performance that relishes the pulsing folk
rhythms.

EMI's plans for Previn look like expanding in reflection of his concert-hall
and television success. The main repertory will still be in the colourful area
where Previn has made his mark most clearly—Tchaikovsky and Prokofiev
both to be represented with complete ballets as well as symphonies, Shostakovich, Rachmaninov. But wisely EMI has plans as well to present Previn
in more central repertory—Beethoven's Fifth Symphony for example and
at least two Mozart Piano Concertos with Previn directing at the keyboard.
It was characteristic of Previn's perennial eagerness to respond to a challenge,
when in August 1972 plans were drawn up literally at a day's notice to
record him playing the piano in partnership with the Yale String Quartet
in Brahms's Piano Quintet. Their live performance at London's Queen
Elizabeth Hall as part of the first season of South Bank Summer Music
organised by Previn as music director was one of the season's great successes,
an example of home music-making writ large. It was timely to have it
translated on to disc.

Inevitably this must be an interim survey, but I cannot think of a more
appropriate record on which to rest the case of Previn, than his bitingly
intense account of Sir William Walton's great dramatic oratorio, *Belshazzar's
Feast*. As I have mentioned earlier, the recording took place on the days
immediately following Previn's live performance with these same forces in
the Royal Festival Hall, and the composer, celebrating his 70th birthday,
was a delighted witness. This is by no means a carbon copy of Walton's
own two recorded performances. Previn tends to adopt slower tempi, and
he uses the extra space to ensure the crispest, most incisive enunciation whether

from singers or players. The very opening demonstrates this, and it is a quality which also marks the beautifully judged performance of Walton's recent *Improvisations on an Impromptu of Benjamin Britten*, the music with which the oratorio is coupled on the record.

Throughout *Belshazzar's Feast* it is striking that the members of the LSO Chorus, rigorously trained by Arthur Oldham, match their instrumental colleagues in the precise shading of dynamic. John Shirley-Quirk is also marvellously focused in the solo role. This is far from being an expansive Royal Albert Hall performance despite the slowish tempi, for there is nothing blurred, nothing left to chance, and dozens of details emerge with extra clarity, whether the xylophone tremolo just before 'Praise ye', the tenor drum that accompanies the writing on the wall or the *Petrushka*-like repeated trumpet notes at the start of the rejoicing after Belshazzar's downfall. That passage of rejoicing in Previn's hands reflects far more clearly than usual the marking 'giocoso'. This is a supremely exuberant performance, which reveals the freedom of enjoyment in a taxing score perfectly mastered.

To see André Previn as a great populariser among conductors is to register his most striking achievement to date. Thanks to the mass media he has leapt the barrier which normally prevents the public at large from warming to a classical conductor. His records so far have tended to concentrate on colourful music, atmospheric and romantic, of the late nineteenth and twentieth centuries, but in every area he has touched he has revealed on record, as in the concert-hall, his astonishing ability to communicate person to person. There is every reason to hope that the process will continue and expand in partnership with the London Symphony Orchestra, bringing us a widened recorded repertory, deepened expression reflecting the spiritual qualities which already in Previn's finest records match his outward-going exuberance.

Christopher Bishop, EMI Recording Manager, discusses a take of 'Belshazzar's Feast' with Previn and John Shirley-Quirk (left). [EMI/G. Macdominic

❧ *Discography* ❧

Compiled by MALCOLM WALKER

Record Categories

Index Letters	Numbers	Example	Type of Record
Roman Capitals	Roman	MGM-C753	Mono LP
Bold Face Capitals	Bold	**SCA5009**	Stereo LP
Italic Capitals	Italic	*MGM-SP1076*	Mono SP (45rpm)
Italic Lower Case	Italic	*mgm-ep627*	Mono EP (45rpm)

† after the number denotes 78rpm record
§ after the number denotes 4-channel LP record

Abbreviations

A.	Argo (UK)	(E) MGM	MGM (UK)	MGM	MGM (USA)
Am. Decca	America Decca (USA)	(E) RCA	RCA (UK)	Philips	Philips (UK)
Angel	Angel (USA)	HMV	HMV (UK)	Polydor	Polydor (UK)
CBS	CBS (USA)	L.	London (USA)	RCA	RCA (UK)
Cont.	Contemporary (USA)	LSO	London Symphony	SFM	Society for Forgotten
D.	Decca (UK)		Orchestra		Music (USA)
(E) CBS	CBS (UK)	MCA	MCA (UK)	Vogue-Cont.	Vogue-Contemporary (UK)

Compiler's Note: The selection of records listed in this discography has been based on those referred to in Edward Greenfield's text. All items conducted by André Previn unless otherwise stated.

1945-6
"PREVIN AT SUNSET"—I got it bad and that ain't good; Body and soul; Sunset in blue; All things you are; Something to live for; Good enough to keep; That old blue magic; Blue skies; I found a new baby; Variations on a theme—with André Previn (piano); assisting musicians include Willie Smith (alto saxophone), Howard McGhee (trumpet), Vido Musso (tenor saxophone), Dave Barbour (guitar)
    Polydor 2460 154

1955
IT'S ALWAYS FAIR WEATHER—soundtrack recording of music from the MGM film with Gene Kelly, Dolores Gray, Dan Dailey, Michael Kidd, Lou Lubin, MGM Studio Orchestra. March, march★; Once upon a time★; Thanks a lot, but no thanks★; Music is better than words★; The time for parting†; Blue Danube (Why are we here?)†; Situation-wise†; I like myself†; Stillman's Gym; Baby you knock me out
    MGM E-3241; (E) MGM MGM868-72†; ★ also issued on (E) MGM *mgm-ep542*; † also issued on (E) MGM *mgm-ep543*

1955
KISS ME KATE—soundtrack recording of music from the MGM film with Kathryn Grayson, Howard Keel, Ann Miller, Tommy Rall, Bobby Van, Bob Fosse, MGM Studio Orchestra. a) Too darn hot; b) So in love; c) We open in Venice; d) Why can't you behave?; e) Were thine that special face; f) Tom, Dick or Harry; g) Wunderbar; h) Always true to you in my fashion; i) I hate men; j) I've come to wive it wealthily in Padua; k) From this moment on; l) Where is the life that late I led?; m) Brush up your Shakespeare; n) So kiss me Kate
    MGM Metro **S525e**/525; (E) MGM MGM-C753; Polydor **2353 062**; e, j and l also issued on (E) MGM MGM-D146; b, d, g, h, n also issued on (E) MGM *mgm-ep627*; a, b also issued on (E) MGM MGM708†/*MGM-SP1076*; g, c, e also issued on (E) MGM MGM709†/*MGM-SP1077*; h, i also issued on (E) MGM MGM710†/*MGM-SP1078*; k, m, n also issued on (E) MGM MGM711†/*MGM-SP1079*

1957
SILK STOCKINGS—soundtrack recording of music from the MGM film with Fred Astaire, Cyd Charisse, Janis Paige, Peter Lorre, Joseph Buloff, Jules Munshin, Carol Richards, The Russians, MGM Studio Orchestra.
Too bad; Paris loves lovers†; Stereophonic sound; It's a chemical reaction, that's all; All of you†; Satin and silk★; Silk stockings; Without love; Fated to be mated; Josephine; Siberia; Red blues; The Ritz roll and rock★; Too bad
    MGM E-3542; (E) MGM MGM-C760; † also issued on (E) MGM MGM963†/45-*MGM963*; ★ also issued on (E) MGM MGM964†/45-*MGM964*

1956 August
"MY FAIR LADY"—free arrangements of music from the Frederick Loewe score. Get me to the church on time; On the street where you live; I've grown accustomed to her face; Wouldn't it be lovely; Ascot Gavotte; Show me; With a little bit of luck; I could have danced all night—with

André Previn (piano), Leroy Vinnegar (bass), Shelly Manne (drums)
> Cont. **7572**/3572; Vogue-Cont. **SCA5009**/LAC12100

1957 June
Capriccio for violin and piano (*William O. Smith*)—with Nathan Rubin (violin), André Previn (piano)
> Cont. **7015**/6001

1958 April
Quartet in A major, Op. 30 (*Chausson*)—with André Previn (piano), members of the Roth String Quartet
> SFM **SFM7014**/1003

1960 December
Piano Quintet, Op. 64 (1938) (*Toch*)—with André Previn (piano), American Art Quartet
> Cont. **8011**/6011

1961
Four Excursions for piano (1945) (*Barber*). Piano Sonata No. 3 (*Hindemith*). Prelude No. 7 for piano (*Frank Martin*)—with André Previn (piano)
> CBS **MS6239**/ML5639

1961
"MACK THE KNIFE and BILBAO SONG" (music of *Kurt Weill*)—Bilbao-Song; Barbara Song; Overture; Seeräuberjenny; Mack the Knife (Moritat); Wie man sich bettet; Unzulänglichkeit—with André Previn (piano), J. J. Johnson (trombone), Red Mitchell (bass), Frank Capp (piano)
> CBS **CS8541**/CL1741; (E) CBS **SBPG62017**/BPG62017; CBS Odyssey **32-16-160260**

1961
Piano Concerto in F★; Rhapsody in Blue (*Gershwin*)—with André Previn (piano), André Kostelantez and his Orchestra
> CBS **CS8286**/CL1495; Philips **SBBL591**/BBL7420; ★ finale of the Concerto also issued on CBS **MS7518**

1961
Mélancolie; Suite française; Presto in B flat (*Poulenc*). Sonatine for piano, Op. 16; Trois pièces (*Roussel*). André Previn (piano), CBS **MS6346**/ML5746

1962
FOUR HORSEMEN OF THE APOCALYPSE— soundtrack recording of music from the MGM film. Main title; Love theme; Resistance; The key; First parting; Paris and Occupation; I've got to see him; Mine for the moment; Chi-Chi's death; Versailles; No divorce; The Four Horsemen
> MGM **SE-3993ST**/E-3993ST; (E) MGM **MGM-CS6053**/MGM-C882

1962
"Together with Love"—with Eileen Farrell (soprano), André Previn (piano) and orchestra
> CBS **CS8720**/CL1920

1962 December
"Piano Pieces for Children"—Variations on "Ah! vous dirai-je maman", K265 (*Mozart*). Six Children's Pieces, Op. 72 (*Mendelssohn*). Two Piano Pieces 1. A Child's Joke; 2. Intermezzo (*Mussorgsky*)—with André Previn (piano)
> CBS **MS6586**/ML5986; (E) CBS **61179**

1963 March
Sinfonia da Requiem, Op. 20 (*Britten*). Red Pony—Suite (*Copland*)—with St Louis Symphony Orchestra
> CBS **MS6583**/ML5983; CBS Odyssey **Y-31016**

1963
Concerto No. 1 for piano, trumpet and orchestra in C minor, Op. 35 (*Shostakovich*)—with André Previn (piano), William Vacchiano (trumpet), New York Philharmonic Orchestra, Leonard Bernstein
> CBS **MS6392**; (E) CBS **SBRG72349-50**/BRG72349-50

1963
"4 TO GO"—No moon at all; Bye Bye blackbird; Life is a ball; It's easy to remember; You're impossible; Oh, what a beautiful morning; I know you oh so well; Intersection; Like someone in love; Dony sing along—with André Previn (piano), Herb Ellis (guitar), Ray Brown (bass), Shelly Manne (drums)
> CBS **CS8818**/CL2018; (E) CBS **SBPG62184**/BPG62184

1963 November
"Piano Pieces for Children"—Piano Pieces for Advanced Children or Retarded Adults; Five Songs with Mendelssohn; Six Technical Studies (which teach you nothing); Eight Studies in Musicology (which will teach you a great deal) (*Godard Lieberson*)—with André Previn (piano)
> CBS **MS6586**/ML5986; (E) CBS **61179**

1964
Trio for violin, cello and piano, Op. 120 (*Fauré*). Piano Trio No. 1 in D minor, Op. 49 (*Mendelssohn*)—with Nathan Roth (violin), Joseph Schuster (cello), André Previn (piano)
> CBS **MS6436**/ML5863

1964 October
Piano Concertos—No. 1 in F sharp minor, Op. 1; No. 4 in G minor, Op. 40 (*Rachmaninov*)—with Leonard Pennario (piano), Royal Philharmonic Orchestra
> RCA **LSC2788**/LM2788; (E) RCA **SB6618**/RB6618

1964 October
Piano Concerto in D flat (*Khachaturian*). Scherzo fantasque (*Bloch*)—with Lorin Hollander (piano), Royal Philharmonic Orchestra
> RCA **LSC2801**/LM2801; (E) RCA **SB6638**/RB6638

1965 August
Symphony No. 5 in D major, Op. 47 (*Shostakovich*)—LSO
> (E) RCA **SB6651**/RB6651; RCA **LSC2866**/LM2866

1965 August
Eight Russian Folksongs, Op. 58 (*Liadov*). Symphony No. 2 in C minor, Op. 17, "Little Russian" (*Tchaikovsky*)—with LSO
> RCA **LSC2884**/LM2884; (E) RCA **SB6670**/RB6670

1966

THOROUGHLY MODERN MILLIE—soundtrack recording of music from the film with Julie Andrews, Carol Channing, John Gavin, Mary Tyler Moore, James Fox with orchestra. Prelude—Thoroughly Modern Millie; Overture; Jimmy; Tapioca; Jazz Baby; Jewish Wedding Song; Intermission medley; Poor Butterfly; Rose of Washington Square; Bacy face; Do it again; Reprise—Thoroughly Modern Millie; Exit music

MCA **MUPS308**/MUP308; Am. Decca **71500**/1500

1966 April

Symphony No. 2 in E minor, Op. 27 (*Rachmaninov*)—with LSO

RCA **LSC2899**/LM2899; (E) **SB6685**/RB6685

1966 April

Sonata for violin and piano (*Debussy*). Violin Sonata in A (*Franck*)—with Erik Friedman (violin), André Previn (piano)

RCA **LSC2907**/LM2907; (E) RCA **SB6688**/RB6688

1966 August

Walton: Symphony No. 1—with LSO

RCA **LSC2927**/LM2927; (E) RCA **SB6691**/RB6691

1966 August

"MUSIC FROM FRANCE FOR OBOE AND ORCHESTRA"—L'horloge de flore (*Françaix*). Symphonie concertante (*Ibert*). Gymnopedies Nos. 1 and 3 (*Satie* orch. *Debussy*)—with John de Lancie (oboe), LSO

(E) RCA **SB6721**; RCA **LSC2945**/LM2945

1967 February

Symphony No. 1 in G minor, Op. 7; Saul and David—prelude to Act 2 (*Nielsen*)—with LSO

RCA **LSC2961**/LM2961; (E) **SB6714**

1967 August

Symphony No. 3 in A minor, Op. 44; Fantasy for orchestra, Op. 7, "The Rock" (*Rachmaninov*)—with LSO

RCA **LSC2990**/LM2990; (E) RCA **SB6729**

1967 August

The Impressario, K486 (English text by Dory Previn) (*Mozart*—with Reri Grist, Judith Raskin (sopranos), Richard Lewis (tenor), Sherill Milnes (baritone), Leo Mackern (narrator) English Chamber Orchestra

RCA **LSC3000**; (E) RCA **SB6764**

1967 May

"Right as the Rain"—with Leontyne Price (soprano), André Previn (piano) and orchestra

RCA **LSC2983**/LM2983

1967 September

Sinfonia Antarctica (*Vaughan Williams*)—with Heather Harper (soprano), Sir Ralph Richardson (speaker), Ambrosian Singers, LSO

RCA **LSC3066**; (E) **SB6736**; (E) RCA **SB6868**

1968 March

Symphony No. 8 (*Vaughan Williams*)—with LSO

RCA **LSC3114**; (E) RCA **SB6769**

1968 March

Three Portraits from "The England of Elizabeth" (suite adapted for concert use by Muir Mathieson) (*Vaughan Williams*)—with LSO

RCA **LSC3280**; (E) RCA **SB6842**

1968 April

Symphony No. 6 in E minor (*Vaughan Williams*)—with LSO

RCA **LSC3114**; (E) RCA **SB6769**

1968 April

Scheherazade, Op. 35; Tsar Sultan—March; Flight of the Bumble Bee (*Rimsky-Korsakov*)—with John Georgiadis (violin), LSO

RCA **LSC3042**; (E) RCA **SB6774**

1968 September

Symphonie espagnole, Op. 21 (*Lalo*). Tzigane (*Ravel*)—with Itzhak Perlman (violin), LSO

RCA **LSC3073**; (E) RCA **SB6800**

1969 March

Symphony No. 4 in F minor; Concerto Accademico★ (*Vaughan Williams*)—with LSO. Item marked ★ with James Oliver Buswell IV (violin)

RCA **LSC3178**; (E) RCA **SB6801**

Item marked † also issued on (E) RCA **SB6868**

1969 March

Der Rosenkavalier—Suite (1945 version); Don Juan, Op. 20; München (Commemorative Waltz—second version) (*Richard Strauss*)—with LSO

RCA **LSC3135**; (E) RCA **SB6838**

1970 February

A Sea Symphony (*Vaughan Williams*)—with Heather Harper (soprano), John Shirley-Quirk (baritone), LSO and Chorus

RCA **LSC3280**; (E) RCA **SER5585**

1970 February

Symphony No. 5 in D; The Wasps—Overture ★ (*Vaughan Williams*)—with LSO

(E) RCA **SB6856**; RCA **LSC3244**

Item marked ★ also issued on (E) RCA **SB6868**

1970 February

Symphony No. 4 in A major, Op. 90, "Italian"; Ruy Blas—overture, Op. 5 (*Mendelssohn*). Symphony No. 1 in D, Op. 25, "Classical" (*Prokofiev*)—with LSO

(E) RCA **SB6847**

1970 March

Piano Concerto in F sharp minor, Op. 1 (*Rachmaninov*)—with Vladimir Ashkenazy (piano), LSO

D. **SXLF6565-7**; L. **CS2311**

1970 June

Violin Concerto in D minor, Op. 47 (*Sibelius*). Violin Concerto

in D major, Op. 35 (*Tchaikovsky*)—with Kyung-Wha Chung (violin), LSO
  D. **SXL6493**; L. **OS6710**

1970 August-September
Overture to a Comedy (*Previn*). A Downland Suite—Minuet (*Ireland*). Overture—Panache (*Chappell*)—with Leicestershire Schools Symphony Orchestra
  A. **ZRG685**

1970 October
Piano Concerto No. 1 in G minor, Op. 25 (*Mendelssohn*)—with Joseph Kalichstein (piano), LSO
  (E) RCA **LSB4053**; RCA **LSC3239**

1970 October
Piano Concerto No. 4 in G minor, Op. 40 (*Rachmaninov*)—with Vladimir Ashkenazy (piano), LSO
  D. **SXLF6565-7**; L. **CS2311**

1970 October
Piano Concerto No. 2 in C minor, Op. 18 (*Rachmaninov*)—with Vladimir Ashkenazy (piano), LSO
  D. **SXLF6565-7**; L. **CS2311**

1971 January
Symphony No. 9 in E minor (*Vaughan Williams*)—with LSO
  RCA **LSC3280**; (E) RCA **SB6842**

1971 January
Pastoral Symphony (*Vaughan Williams*)—with LSO
  (E) RCA **SB6861**; RCA **LSC3281**

1971 February
Guitar Concerto (*Villa-Lobos*)—with Julian Bream (guitar), LSO
  RCA **LSC3231**; (E) RCA **SB6852**; slow movement only contained in (E) RCA **SER5638-42**

1971 March
Piano Concerto No. 3 in D minor, Op. 30 (*Rachmaninov*)—with Vladimir Ashkenazy (piano), LSO
  D. **SXLF6565-7**; L. **CS2311**

1971 May
Concerto in F minor for bass tuba and orchestra (*Vaughan Williams*)—with John Fletcher (bass tuba), LSO
  RCA **LSC3281**; (E) RCA **SB6861**, (E) RCA **SB6868**

1971 May
Sitar Concerto (*Shankar*)—with Ravi Shankar (sitar), LSO
  HMV **ASD2752**; Angel **S36806**

1971 June
Rhapsody in Blue★; An American in Paris; Piano Concerto in F★ (*Gershwin*)—with LSO. Items marked ★ with André Previn (piano)
  HMV **ASD2754**; Angel **S36810**

1971 November
Rhapsody on a theme of Rachmaninov, Op. 43 (*Rachmaninov*)—with Vladimir Ashkenazy (piano), LSO
  D. **SXLF6565-7**; CL. **CS2311**

1971 November
Alexander Nevsky—Cantata, Op. 78 (*Prokofiev*)—with Anna Reynolds (mezzo-soprano), LSO and Chorus
  HMV **ASD2800**; Angel **S36843**

1971 November
"LSO GALA"—Candide Overture (*Bernstein*). Fantasia on "Greensleeves"★ (*Vaughan Williams*). Rumanian Rhapsody, Op. 11 No. 1 (*Enesco*)—with LSO
  HMV **ASD2784**; Item marked ★ also issued on HMV **SEOM12**

1971 November
Guitar Concerto (*Previn*)—with John Williams (guitar), LSO
  (E) CBS **73060**

1972 January
A London Symphony (*Vaughan Williams*)—with LSO
  (E) RCA **SB6860**; RCA **LSC3282**

1972 January
Concierto del Sur (*Ponce*)—with John Williams (guitar), LSO
  (E) CBS **73060**

1972 March
Belshazzar's Feast (*Walton*)—with John Shirley-Quirk (baritone), LSO and Chorus
  HMV **SAN324/4Q-SAN324**§

1972 May
Improvisations on an Impromptu by Benjamin Britten (*Walton*)—with LSO
  HMV **SAN324/4Q-SAN324**§

1972 May
The Nutcracker—Ballet, Op. 71 (*Tchaikovsky*)—with LSO
  HMV **SLS834**

1972 August
Piano Quintet in F minor, Op. 34 (*Brahms*)—with André Previn (piano), Yale String Quartet
  HMV (awaiting release)

1972 August
Violin Concerto in D (*Stravinsky*). Violin Concerto (*Walton*)—with Kyung-Wha Chung (violin), LSO
  D. (awaiting release)

1972/73
1812 Overture, Op. 49; Marche Slav, Op. 31 (*Tchaikovsky*)—with LSO
  HMV (awaiting release)

The following are also awaiting release by HMV:
Symphony No. 5 in C minor, Op. 67 (*Beethoven*)—with LSO
Symphony No. 2 in E minor, Op. 27 (*Rachmaninov*)—with LSO
Symphony No. 8 (*Shostakovich*)—with LSO

January 1973

96

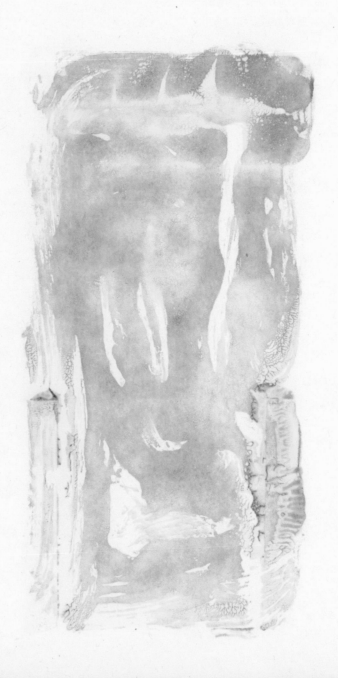